A Northwoods Window

Robert Treuer

Voyageur Press

Printed in the United States of America
90 91 92 93 94 5 4 3 2 1

Library of Congress Cataloging-in-Publication Data

Treuer, Robert.
    A Northwoods window / Robert Treuer,
        p.   cm.
    ISBN 0-89658-123-3
    1. Treuer, Robert.   2. Naturalists — Minnesota — Biography.
    3. Natural history — Minnesota.   I. Title.
    QH31.T744A3   1990
    508.776 — dc20   90-30437
                                                                      CIP

Published by Voyageur Press, Inc.
P.O. Box 338
123 North Second Street
Stillwater, MN 55082 U.S.A.
In Minn 612-430-2210
Toll-free 800-888-9653

Cover illustration by Craig MacIntosh
Cover design by Lou Gordon

Distributed in Canada by Whitecap Books
Vancouver/Toronto

Voyageur Press books are also available at discounts for quantities for educational, fundraising, premium, or sales-promotion use. For details contact the marketing manager. Please write or call for our free catalog of publications.

Dedicated to Steve Isaacs and Robert Girouard,
editors of integrity and insight,
with gratitude for their faith in my work

Acknowledgments

All chapters of this book have appeared in much the same form in the *Minneapolis Star* (later the *Star Tribune*), the *Bemidji Pioneer,* and the *Brainerd Dispatch.* Some have appeared in *The Washington Post, Chicago Sun Times, Milwaukee Journal,* and the *International Falls Daily Journal.*

Contents

Preface: Aneen

Aneen is the Ojibwe *hello*.

The stories and essays of *A Northwoods Window* are to entertain you; as one looks out a window to observe the spectacle of life, so can you look out through these pages — at the man who stood in the middle of a busy highway to escort a turtle to safety, at the blueberry raiding party, the mud-mired census takers, and at the long-sought beavers who finally return to flood the family. But windows look inward, too. And most of these chapters raise questions of values and ethics. Does stewardship of the land connote some kind of dominance over creation? How can a mortal human own, or steward, immortal creation? Why is a solitary turtle important? Are my neighbor's blueberries bluer than the ones in my woods?

As a window serves two functions, allowing one to look out and letting the outside in, so do these stories and essays.

Instruction by storytelling is the traditional Indian way of communicating meanings. Our family has become more traditionally Indian in our spiritual life over the years, and in some ways *A Northwoods Window* reflects these evolving values, as in the beaver chapters.

I was an adult when a man, with his extended family, adopted me. He did this in a traditional way because he had come to love me as a son. His family, his village, and his reservation enfolded me. He and other elders became willing to share teachings and I was drawn ever deeper into their rich, spiritual lode. To feel as one with the smallest pebble and with the distant star has brought harmony and peace into my life, and intense appreciation and enjoyment of life and creation.

ANEEN

My childhood years were turbulent. I grew up in Vienna amid fascist violence and then Nazi persecution. Fragments of my family escaped the Holocaust, some of us to the United States. After World War II military service, followed by college, I became a labor union activist in Wisconsin, a teacher in northern Minnesota, and a community organizer in service of Indian communities. I took a government job in Washington for a while but my heart took me home again. I have been a writer and teacher since, living on our tree farm on the rivulet Mississippi near Bemidji.

A few nights before my adoption, my father-to-be and other village elders began my instruction. The first teaching was that I must accept what is given completely and without thought of reciprocity or recompense. The second corollary teaching was that when I shared or gave, I must do so freely without expectation of return. Both giving and getting must be entirely free and whole hearted, without strings attached.

The loan of life is a gift I receive and which I accept completely. Teaching and writing are my sharing.

1 Return of the Beavers

When I first acquired the deserted farm that has now become our home and a tree farm more than thirty years ago, beavers were sparse. Here and there some of the many lodges were occupied. Nearby farmboys and a handful of trappers — and modest fur prices — kept the population in some sort of balance.

I heard stories of the beavers' mischief, flooding roads and inundating farmlands, and of neighbors dynamiting dams and trapping them. This sounded needlessly vicious to me, an extreme extension of the ethos of man shaping the world to his convenience at the cost of ecological balance and, ultimately, environmental sanity. My neighbors did not argue and merely arched their eyebrows, implying that I would learn in time.

The number of beavers declined, until the sighting of an occasional stray in search of terrain and companionship became a rarity. Lakes and creeks were abundant, and the growth of aspen and other foods sought by beavers was rampant, so that it seemed a shame not to have more of them around. This thought came to me often during drought years when the water levels dropped and the fire hazard was severe. Then the retained water backed up behind the beaver dams would have been very welcome; but there were no occupied lodges nearby.

They returned inexplicably in modest numbers, and hard on their heels came the trappers. I posted my land, tried to locate the trappers who came up the river and overland, whose traps and tracks I found but whose ghostlike comings and goings eluded me. I sprang the traps, which they reset. I removed the traps and, one day when I was away at work, they sank the swimming raft floating on barrels on my lake with gunshot.

1

Then the beavers were gone again, the last lodge trapped out, and the conflict became passé.

*   *   *

Game wardens and foresters at the state Department of Natural Resources listen sympathetically to my pleading for the transplanting of beavers into my denuded lake.

"If you have nuisance beavers somewhere and have to trap them, you can put them in my lake," I offer.

"Live trapping is very time consuming, very costly," the game warden says. "We don't do that anymore."

Where absolutely necessary, licenses are issued to local residents to trap the beavers, to kill them, and to take their furs. Ordinarily, though, it is a matter of gritting teeth, planning and building roads and bridges with the possibility of beaver dams in mind, and sometimes installing sluices that have to be opened in the mornings and closed at night, thus baffling the nocturnal beavers as they seek the "leak." No other effective baffles or controls have yet been found.

"You're sure you want beavers?" the game warden asks, a tone of disbelief in his voice.

"Certainly!" (I tend to be emphatic to my eventual regret.)

"We'll call you if we ever have any," they say, but they never do.

The beavers return in numbers and suddenly. We watch with delight as the old lodge on our lake is renovated, expanded, refurbished, and likewise two lodges on the next lake. It seems to me that their appetites are modest and their incursions for building materials well within the provender of our woods, without undue damage.

However, they dam the outlet of the lake and the water rises ever higher, far beyond their needs. I open the dam to lower the water level, and they rebuild it bigger and better by next morning. Woven into the dam structure, amid branches and clumps of mud, is lake-bottom debris: cow and pig bones (I had heard tales of farm animals getting mired, then being lost in the silt of the lakeshore long ago), broken glass and pieces of some particularly garish blue and white dinnerware. I do not know the source of these shards, which my wife Peggy refers to as Blue Willow. ("Let them haul up the pieces, maybe we can glue them together and wind up with a complete set," she says, but I fail to see the humor; somehow blue and white pieces of plate clash with my image of northwoods wilderness.)

Our son David finds an antique bottle embedded in the dam, and Peggy mentions that this could have some value. People collect old bottles. (A grievous development because David has the instincts of a banker.) "If we open up the dam just a little bit each night," David suggests, "they might bring up some more old bottles. I can wash them out and sell them!" The beavers now have a champion and David has visions of trained beavers ransacking lake bottoms in search of antique glassware.

A second and third opening of the dam only results in a bigger and better dam the next day. I arrive one morning to find it not only rebuilt, but across the top of it a sheet of plastic neatly anchored with branches and mud. I had lost that sheet months before in a windstorm. So much for beavers in the wilds; ours are scavengers pure and simple, too lazy to cut their own dam materials and unearthing human debris and middens as an unsightly labor-saving device. I give up for the season.

*   *   *

It is a long winter with an unusual amount of snow. The arrival of warm weather and spring runoff sees the beavers re-emerge, their numbers augmented by progeny who have to be taught dam building.

One of my neighbors maintains that beavers react to the sound of running water, taking this as a breach of their dikes. If this is true, this spring's record runoff is driving the beavers to heroic efforts. A tote road, kept open for fire control access, is flooded. The lake expands in size. The children's swimming hole up the creek is deep enough for me. The greening trees around the periphery of the lake turn brown as waterlogged roots rot and die. The emerald lake is no longer ringed in green, but by brown and sere skeletons of birch, cedar, pine, and aspen. Then the access to the building site for our new house becomes waterlogged and, finally, impassable.

The return of the beavers has produced an unsightly array of dead and dying trees, inconvenience, and impediment to our use of the land. In the larger framework of a wilderness eco-system, with its long-range cycles and episodes, the beavers' presence and alteration of the environment are productive and necessary. On the smaller scale of our land, coexistence—so ardently sought by me for so long, and now so greedily supported by David—becomes a seeming impossibility.

Live-trapping *is* difficult and time consuming.

Operating a sluice installed in their dam—opening it in the morning and closing it in the evening—becomes a major chore and represents a substantial installation expense.

Dynamiting the dam gives only temporary relief and rarely drives out the beavers. Trapping and killing still go against the grain.

I amuse friends by describing the recipes I intend to use for Christmas dinner of roast beaver, and my plans to make a beaver coat for my wife. ("But I want a store-bought coat!" Peggy protests.)

Meanwhile our house-building project is slowed to a creeping stall, no alternative sites being feasible. More trees around the lake are dying. I grit my teeth while they whet theirs. I contemplate beavercide while my children, groomed and conditioned to a love of wildlife over the years, tell me that the young beavers are "cute," and of their antics at close range.

"And remember the bottles, Dad," adds David.

An engineer is coming over to advise us on the cost of building a bridge.

2 The OPEC Avenger

A neighbor, in northwoods idiom, is someone with whom one shares a sense of community, a sense of commonality where public concerns arise. In a city this might be confined by a block, or one street, or a group of blocks. In the northwoods the distances are greater, and the dimensions slightly different because we need each other more intensely, sometimes more dramatically, for the support that in a metropolis is within reach of telephone. Steve Bergstrom is both friend and neighbor, though we live fifteen miles apart.

I drive into his yard and find him standing atop a mountainous woodpile, thumbing his nose at OPEC.

"The oil cartel can go to hell!" he shouts. "I'm going to be warm this winter!"

His youngsters smile and shrug it off. They have heard it many times while helping to cut, split, and stack countless cords of firewood. They have even made peace with their father's infatuation with his monstrous chain saw, his preoccupation with the proper angle for the file to sharpen the chain, his compulsive shopping for a pickaroon with a tempered steel head to pull the logs to the sawing trough. His wife Carol has become complaisant about sawdust and woodchips cascading from his clothes, and tells me not to worry as the cuffs on my pants disgorge debris on their carpet, mementos from my own woodcutting.

Huge winter woodpiles have become commonplace throughout the woodland belt across the country. Hereabouts hardwoods are still plentiful, though no one knows how long the supply will last. Overnight, everyone has become a connoisseur, a *cognoscente*, of the various brands and types of wood furnaces, stoves, and space heaters.

"I got an Ashley; whatchyu got?"

"Bunyan."

"Um."

A whole new vocabulary, set of code words, dialogue. Get two tyros started on the virtues and vices of chain saw brands, and it will bring a new dimension to the English language. It is more than a craze; it has become an overnight standard. Secondary heating units using wood often sell out upon delivery to the stores, and new housing usually features wood and other fuel systems in combination.

A whole new cottage industry has arisen in welding and machine shops where a wild variety of wood stoves are being turned out. One such manufacturer advertises its product as The OPEC Avenger.

Wood heat went out with the other conveniences (and hard work) of life a few decades ago. My wife's mother recalls the joy with which the old wood-burning kitchen range, complete with warming oven and water reservoir, was taken to the village dump and interred. It went the way of the kerosene lanterns, the barrel stove. All are gone beyond retrieval and we wish we had them now.

Even after the necessity for wood fuel had disappeared, a lot of people fed fireplaces; a few hardy souls used their barrel stoves for the smell, the ethos of it, if not from economic necessity or habit. There was also the sensuous thrill of the particular bone-penetrating warmth of a wood fire while relishing the smell and the visual benefit: What better trigger for daydreams and fantasies than the licking flames dancing before you?

Now it's a different story.

The Bergstroms have two wood space heaters, the use of which will keep their oil furnace idle most of the time. We have a wood space heater that furnishes 50 percent of our house-heating needs this winter; the new house we are building will have a central wood furnace and supplementary heat from another source, while our kitchen wood range will supplement the regular one. Other neighbors have different combinations: fireplaces with air-circulating systems; and a couple with double-decked barrel stoves in which smoke and heat are ducted from the bottom barrel, where the wood is burned, into a second barrel on its top, and then to the chimney. It is an old-fashioned remedy recently rediscovered and works well if you can put up with the direct, intense heat and the energy loss which are concomitants of barrel stoves. Yet another innovation places the double-decker barrel stove into a cement block building or stall adjacent to the house, or nearby; the heat is then brought into the house through ducts.

*   *   *

The Bergstroms cut some of the wood on their land, and buy most from a local logger. We use the same tactics, though the supply of good firewood is thinning out and I have no intention of denuding my land of hardwoods over the space of a few years, knowing they will take many decades to regenerate back to firewood size.

Actually the Bergstroms' house is surrounded by a two- or three-year supply of firewood that Steve vows to protect with his life.

The way that happened is quite normal. They had made arrangements with the logger for three truckloads of dry hardwood, seasoned at least a year after cutting. Each truckload produces several cords (a cord is four feet high, four feet wide, and eight feet long). Three truckloads would be sufficient for one, perhaps two years. When the wood was not delivered several months later and the logger did not return their telephone calls, they ordered three loads from someone else. All six arrived, plus a seventh, plus some "extra" everyone had thrown in, perhaps in response to Carol's telephone distress. Now you wouldn't want to see all those nice kids freezing to death this winter, would you? The Bergstroms received very ample loads.

The lag in delivery time wasn't just a matter of a logging truck breaking down and the long wait for parts, nor of the wetness of the access roads to cutting areas where the wood had been stacked. The loggers have to go farther and look more assiduously. Yesteryear's drag on the market is tomorrow's scarce find—that is, if you want to burn seasoned hardwood, which has many times the fuel, and heating, content of softwoods such as pine. Even plentiful popple (aspen) does not make for very good firewood and ranks far down the scale from birch, elm, maple, oak, ash, and others.

One can't help wondering about the wood supplies for future years, especially as one passes mountains of firewood in towns, and not only in rural yards. On a recent network television newscast filmed in New England, I spotted quite a few piles of firewood in the town. It looked like Bemidji.

Hardwood seedlings are difficult to obtain in quantity, are costly, and I don't know of anyone planting hardwoods on a large scale as we have done over the years with pine.

Even *if* seedlings in quantity were available, it would require more than my lifetime to produce trees of firewood size, much less replenish what I propose to burn. Softwoods grow much faster, but in addition to being inefficient fuel they coat the stove or furnace quickly with accumulations of soot, creosote, and other residues, however well designed the apparatus.

I don't think we will run out of hardwood to burn right away, and try to assure Steve Bergstrom that he won't have to sit on top of his woodpile, shotgun in hand, to protect hearth and home from the theft of his bulwark against OPEC. But there is no question the commodity is becoming harder to find and going up in price, whether you buy it or do it yourself— driving longer and farther, working longer and harder.

And we have to look into the planting and regeneration of the bounty we use. I don't want my children or grandchildren to have to sit on top of *their* woodpiles, or to have to lock them up as some folks now do with their gas tanks.

*   *   *

It does not seem possible that our forests could vanish. But ancient Greece and Rome were heavily wooded, in places with giant oaks. The great forests retained moisture and held the soil. Then the forests were cut: rulers of the world need navies and farmlands, and growing populations require firewood. Goats and other domestic animals grazed the hillsides; then rains washed away the soil. Great portions of Greece and Italy became barren rockland, and countryside that produced the golden bough is perpetually desolate.

It is possible. Will we allow it to happen here?

3 Macho Hunter

The first couple days of deer season are usually a dead loss because I like to mosey around the woods quietly, tracking and stalking, playing deer games, and the city hunters who board at a nearby farm have a different approach. Their boisterous shouts echo over the township, they fire their rifles wildly before and after each drive, and their beer cans could stock a medium-sized recycling center, if only they were picked up. Yesterday morning they overslept, made up for it by an extra loud drive through the woods, all fifteen in top voice, but they had forgotten to post standers. My neighbor Chuck was sitting in the woods and saw them emerge looking puzzled, then chagrined; they did not even see him.

I use those first two days to criss-cross the land, intersecting it east-west then north-south at quarter mile intervals and getting a feel for how many deer there are in the area, and what their movements tend to be. What are they feeding on at this time? Where are they bedding down? So long as I move without haste, nearby deer will quietly slip around me and resume their daytime naps, and I in turn can do some serious hunting after the temporary turmoil has subsided.

Last night's fusillade, augmented by firecrackers, has given me notice that the visitors are about to depart, and I set out this morning with relief and relish. The dog, part husky, is safely in the house so that he can't romp through the woods with me — he bounds through the brush like a jackrabbit, with occasional high leaps. I leave him looking wistful and shut the door firmly in his face.

It is still, gray, and cold. When daylight is full the temperature will drop further, before rising to the thawing point later in the day. That means frozen leaves crackling underfoot. The house behind me is dark save for the kitchen window, where the single light will welcome my rising family and point their unerring way to the coffee pot which I have left half full. White smoke drifts up uncertainly from the chimney, refusing to tell me which way the wind will blow. So be it.

I hunch into myself in the chill as I pad along the trail, aiming myself in the direction of the crossing deerpaths I have chosen. This is the morning stand I use each year, but I claim each time that it has been scientifically derived after taking a census of the deer. I like it because it is set among very big pines that were too small at the turn of the century when the loggers came through, and have somehow been overlooked ever since. The place looks out over a marsh and tamarack swamp, and as I perch on the hillside I can enjoy both forest and lowland, and can hear the loons nearby (and they still have not left). Overhead I can see the scattered flights of ducks and geese heading south. It *is* idyllic and the anticipation is antidote to the cold as I make my way.

Five minutes' hike away from the house, our black and white cat emerges from the grass, plump from his night's hunt, hungry for affection. He wraps himself around my legs and purrs—it sounds very loud—and then yowls as I continue to walk on. He is not a Siamese, but he *is* vocal. I squat, try to discourage with motions and a not-too-gentle shove, and he peers into the rifle barrel.

What a temptation! Felinicide! I can get revenge for all the times he has awakened me in the middle of the night! For the times I've had to feed him (which Tony and David swore they would do religiously if only I would let them have that cute kitten). He yowls again and I wish him into the cookpot of the recently departed hunters.

I tell him mentally: "There are four does and one buck in these woods—be quiet and it will bring you greater rewards! Just think of all the venison!" But ESP doesn't work, and he comes along, occasionally serenading me as we go. I consider taking him home and setting out again, but it is getting much lighter and I will miss the best time of the morning if I do. Maybe he'll curl up and go to sleep once we get to the stand.

We arrive. I am exercised, he is exercising, and the crackle of the frozen leaves under his stamping paws sounds explosive. Then a red squirrel awakens and scolds. Usually this squirrel gives me a few blasts, *pro forma*, and goes on to more important things. It is what red squirrels do when deer pass by, and I have come to listen to them for advance notice of approaching deer. Not today, when he is in a high dither about the cat and continues to scold. A pine cone comes thudding down, then another, as the squirrel escalates the conflict.

What happened to still hunting? To the time I could silently make my way to this spot, the deer coming along later, waking a sleeping partridge? Where is the silence of the great northwoods? I am having trouble with noise pollution!

The cat gives up. He had tried to curl up and sleep, twice he attempted my lap amid discouraging hand motions, and now he stalks away stiff-leggedly, singing as he goes. The squirrel follows him.

It is broad daylight and there are sunshafts through the trees. In the distance the die-hard loons are greeting the day, and my ears are acclimating to the normal sounds of the forest. A good fifty, sixty feet away is a bunch of chickadees fluttering, feeding, chirping. I get the first intimations of warmth, then the wind rises. From the south! I'm in the wrong place. A south wind means that deer, as they wake and head out to feed, will come out of the tamarack swamp at the opposite end. I've had a pleasant morning stand, even if I had guessed wrong—it's happened before, and likely will again.

I rise slowly, restore circulation in my numb legs, and think of walking home for more coffee before stalking. The boys will have left for school—I did not hear them today as I often do, but recognized the growl of the bus motor in the distance at some time past. I set out on the trail.

At the foot of the hill the cat and I meet again. I am an empty-handed hunter. He is eating the squirrel.

4 The Thermal "I" of the Beholder

"We're having typical fall weather," I write a friend. "Several inches of snow, frozen lakes, and chilblains."

The posting of banns legitimizing winter is a month away. Has our marriage of Minnesotans and climate been by common law, a *sub rosa* affair that necessitates the pretense that it isn't really cold, that we are not really freezing? How can the wind chill be minus twenty-seven and the calendar says it is still autumn? I have often been struck by the paradox that legally sanctioned winter begins when the days get longer and the temperature colder. What kind of marriage is this?

Faraway friends and relatives consider it insanity that I live in the northwoods by choice, and that I like it. I bolster them in their view, in part because I do not want to encourage overpopulation and we who live here prize the space, and in part because I can't dissuade them from their convictions anyhow. Opinions are more dearly held than scientific fact, or emotional and spiritual need.

I have my own pernicious ways of exaggerating the weather reports in conversation and correspondence, making casual mention of the chill factor or the month-long subzero spell, as though it were an everyday occurrence. The trick is to be matter of fact about it. The truth is that I get just as cold as my friends in warmer climes; but like other northerners, I ease into it, and get acclimated. And usually the transition to the cold weather is gradual, in spells and spurts, and it is a rare winter that descends overnight.

It is a blustery early December day, not what you would call a blizzard, but the wind is out of the northwest at about twenty-five miles an hour, driving the light snow and making it seem more than it really is. A few inches of snow have gathered on the ground over the past two weeks, giving a softness to each step. It is a day when I relish a walk in the woods. While it is true that the wind drives the fifteen-degree temperature to subzero, the forest and the undulations of the land will shield me.

Earlier in the season I might have been tempted to overdress for the occasion, but now I am somewhat accustomed, body and mind having accepted the fact that it is colder than it was at the beginning of autumn. Long johns and dungarees; cotton socks and one pair of wool socks; T-shirt, sweater, and wool shirt. I am ready for the knitted wool cap, jacket, and knee-high gum boots that serve me nine months of the year in wet or snowy weather. It will get much colder before I escalate to heavier clothing. My main purpose now is to have a double layer of clothing, which allows the body to breathe and to ventilate, much as Indian and Inuit clothing in the old days used to work.

Going out the door, I finally remember to take the emergency kit and put it in the car. I have been remiss in not doing this earlier. The battered suitcase, which will stay in the car until warm weather, contains a complete outfit of heavy clothing, an old pair of extra boots, matches, a candy bar, and a sleeping bag. I've needed it only twice in over twenty years, but both times, on desolate roads in bitter cold, I was glad to have had it. Once, near Nett Lake, a large buck lunged out of dense woods and into my slow-moving car. The impact was enough to send the car into a ditch, and me on foot to seek help: The embankment was too steep and I could not shovel and drive out. The other occasion was more tragic. Rounding a corner in the early morning of one of those rare minus fifty degree days, I saw an inert form in the middle of the pavement. No car, no tire marks, just a body sprawled face down; its warmth had melted an oval of snow, which had then frozen. He was an old-timer, a lumberjack who had remained to farm, living a recluselike old age. It turned out later that he had left home late the evening before to go visiting in town, but had taken a wrong turn. Discovering his mistake, he tried to turn around in someone's driveway, had driven into a ditch and been unable to extricate the car. Then he began to walk, not dressed for the arctic cold, just a sheepskin vest over his regular clothing. He walked past two lighted homes before collapsing and dying in the middle of the pavement. No cars had come by all night.

In our machine-dependent lives, we come to ignore the elements and nature, plunging from our warm homes into warm cars, then into a warm store, forgetting what we have known. Is this what happened? A lapse in his lifetime knowledge and respect of nature? Reliant on mechanical contraptions and devices that shield one from life? I often remember the dying of the old lumberjack, and I keep the memory green so that I may not come to take modern conveniences for granted, and so that I retain a healthy respect for the world in which I live. While I can only speculate on some of the whys and hows of his death, I am sure he did not intend to die that night. He had a large sum of money in his pocket.

*   *   *

I scud through the snow, its softness silencing my steps, the wind dissipating the small noises as my jacket brushes against the branches. Ahead, huddled on the ground against hazelbrush, a partridge bobs its head, apparently discerning my moving shape. It cannot hear my coming, amid the sound of the wind, and its already poor vision is further diminished by the speeding snowflakes, the crystals caroming in the wind. I get within seven feet before the bird reluctantly flies away, beating awkwardly among the trees in search of a safe roost.

Few animals move about at the height of a wind like this, and I can appreciate their hunkering down as I feel it burn against the right side of my face. It is not only the discomfort that keeps them in hiding, I suspect, but that they are so vulnerable, unable to hear or see danger, the wind velocity even diminishing and distorting odors. Their disadvantage is my advantage. A deer has curled up right on the trail, where runways cross, bedding down in the pineduff in a shallow depression, its body heat melting the snow. The deer is not aware of my approach, and I debate whether to circumvent it and leave it in peace, or to approach to see how close I can get. Curiosity wins. At thirty feet downwind from it, the deer's head is raised, the ears twitching as it cranes around. I am fifteen feet downwind before the doe rises, lopes a few steps, then walks away.

There are no rabbit tracks where ordinarily their runways would be full of fresh signs. But the red squirrels are busy and about, though not inclined to scold me, and the small rodents are active; I see their fresh tunnels and footmarks even as the snow covers them. Among sheltered trees chickadees and nuthatches have business as usual. A few days ago on a similar walk I had come upon a flock of excited blue jays bedeviling an arctic owl perched high in a popple tree. The blue jays were screeching, diving at the owl, which finally rose and flew away, coasting among the trees.

The cloud cover must be thinning, harbinger of weather change, but wind and snowflakes continue unabated. I can tell because sunlight suddenly blazes through a patch of woods, a window in the sky admitting golden light, a gothic illumination among the pillars of the trees. Even the snowflakes are tinted, gilded rockets in the cold wind. Then the clouds close over, pulling the shades.

The pines that were momentarily bright green are bluer and blacker now, the bark so briefly hued red and pale gray is darker. It had been a very brief interlude, that visit from the sunlight, but then so is my walk in the winter woods in the wind and the snow. Like the visit of the sun, my walk invigorates and illuminates my spirit, and I am content to turn back, retracing my steps.

5 The Tree Farmer's Christmas Tree

Even a tree farmer can have problems getting a Christmas tree, and the time has come to gather the clan for the annual outing. If the selection were to be a democratic event, the six of us would erupt from the doorway and scatter in six different directions. Tony said that he found "the perfect balsam" in the southwest forty. David insists that he has his eye on a much better one elsewhere. The twins, too young to vocalize their choices, would head out at random anyhow, like bits of mercury. Peggy is mustering arguments, good lawyer that she is, about the advantages of Norway pine in the east plantation. I have my eye on a spruce, but keep the information to myself, counting it a momentary blessing that my three grown sons and their families have not joined us as yet, because I am sure they would have some notions too.

"Let's build a bonfire on the sledding hill," I propose.

"Good, I've got the makings for s'mores," says Peggy.

The hill is central to everyone's wishes, provides plenty of diversions, and I hope that the food will be a common denominator, a bribe to agreement. We set out in the brisk wind, the sky pale blue, the winter forest showing many shades of green. The twins' blue plastic sled contrasts to the white snow, and they crow happily, scooping up snow as we pull them along. I ignore their eating the stuff, having accepted the futility of unenforceable commands.

Christmas tree season begins in November, with the family closing ranks into a unified front as passing deer hunters covet our plantation. We aren't the kind of tree farmers who raise Christmas trees. Those would need to be pruned and sheared yearly, otherwise they would be too bushy to fit in most living rooms. We have examined the costs of pruning and shearing, of cutting and bundling, and transporting the trees, and found this type of operation to be marginal. The truth is that we prefer the aesthetic and ethical values of reforestation, of environmental regeneration evidenced by returning wildlife and wildflowers as a setting wherein we live our lives and rear our children.

But deer hunters and others bent on latrociny never seem inclined to go to a dense stand and steal a tree there. They usually practice their piracy close to the road in an open spot, taking a bushy tree where it can least be spared. Poor soil and erosion are responsible for the dying of the seedlings in what now shows as somewhat open area, precisely where the few remaining trees are needed most. And that is where the occasional thefts take place. So the family that prizes independence and differences unites, and even our dog, a true Caspar Milquetoast despite his fierce appearance, senses that some show of viciousness is desired. He does a few practice growls which leave our cat unimpressed.

The United Front is down on thieves, especially those few who climb a forty- or fifty-year-old spruce and cut the top off. The decapitated remainder is usually ruined. Fortunately, these instances are rare and Tony and David are particularly vigilant even if the dog is not.

What is more difficult to handle is that our family and friends, seeing us reside amid several hundred thousand trees, take it for granted that we want to share our bounty. Our expanded family is large and getting larger, and while I love visiting with distant relatives, with third and fourth cousins and with friends of friends, I feel clutchy when the conversation turns to the tree farm, how nice the trees look, and the oncoming holiday season.

*　　　*　　　*

The fire blazes and crackles, undeterred by the melted snow at its base. We have a plentiful supply of brush and slashings, hauled there during autumn and early winter walks for those sledding times. A similar fuel pile is down at the lake, in case the ice is blown clear of snow and we can go skating, which has not happened yet this year. We enjoy the business of the fire, not really needing the warmth because the work of building it has kept us warm. An outdoor fire has its own atavistic ethos, its smells and sounds evocative of other times, evocative perhaps of something primal in us. We needlessly admonish the twins to not get too close; the heat of the fire is a more effective disciplinarian than our exhortations.

Tony and David are rolling in the snow, and Micah and Megan emulate them, squealing and laughing, their eyes shining, their cheeks ruddy. I wish I were young enough to enjoy, to feel good about getting snow down my neck.

Peggy has disappeared into the plantation, and we catch up as she critically examines a Norway pine on the hoof.

"That's too bushy," says Tony.

"Too big," David agrees.

"Well, the branches we cut off can be used in a wreath!" But Peggy knows she is just arguing for the sake of it; she makes beautiful wreaths of balsam and cedar, never of Norway.

We find a patch of princess pine, and pick some for wreaths and decoration. I go on a private safari for bittersweet growing near the marsh, the bare pale brown and gray vines ending in clusters of bright red and orange berries.

Back at the fire we roast marshmallows, squish them between chocolate and graham crackers. Hunger has brought us together. Megan has a passion for chocolate, but can't separate it from the rest of the concoction. Micah, indiscriminate, uses both hands to shove everything within reach into his mouth.

I wander over to the spruce, look at it speculatively from all sides, and sadly shake my head.

"That looks pretty good," Peggy says. "What's the matter with it?"

"Thin on one side."

"But Dad, that'll be just fine turned to the corner!" Tony has joined us.

"The top is a little spindly."

David has an answer: "You always cut some off the top to fit the star!"

We cut the tree and head for home, through the forest we have planted and through the woodland patches of natural growth. They shield us from the wind, and we are surrounded by the echoing sounds of the children's voices.

6 Resolution

The major Christmas gift for Tony and David is a pair of snow-shoes for each. At ten and nine respectively, the boys are big enough and these can last a lifetime. Hardwood frames, raw-hide lacing, the old-fashioned kind, and hard to find. Most stores these days carry them, if at all, made of plastic in part or in whole.

We sit on the floor, looping on the bindings. I have had to repair my own leather bindings and replace them as they wore, cracked, and gave out.

"One winter day, when your older brothers were high school age, and the snow was piled several feet deep, Frank De-Clusin showed up at the door. He had snowshoed all the way from his home to have someone to play with."

"Frank-who-owns-the-horses? He lives five miles away!"

"That's right. He had no car, and he wanted company, so he came cross country."

"That's a long way," Tony says.

"Not if you're lonesome and want to visit a friend. About two hours one way, maybe a little less. Now look here, you slip your toe over this strap and under that one. Then you tighten the two straps—the one over the instep, and the other behind the heel. And you never step on the cross brace, that wooden slat, or you'll break it."

"Can I try mine on?" David is anxious.

"Only on the snow, where the snowshoe can sink in a little bit without damaging the webbing."

They'll learn, take their tumbles, get caught in the brush. Then there'll come an exhilarating moment when they go scud-

23

ding along, catch the rhythm, and relish the freedom of movement atop the deep snow through the woods and marshes.

Snowshoes are not a luxury item here, but a necessity if you trap or work in the deep woods. To me they are a necessity not so much for the work, but for my year-round and almost daily forays into the woods. My own snowshoes are scarred and worn, and long overdue for a new coat of varnish or polyurethane; I'm not a good example to my young sons. However neglected, my snowshoes and I have an intimate relationship. The left one has a very slight squeak that has defied countless applications of neat's-foot oil to the bindings. The right one tends to trail at the tail, making a soft "scuff-scuff" sound. This is also a matter of adjusting the binding, a small matter on which we have not gotten together over the years, but nothing to seriously impair an otherwise satisfactory partnership.

*　　　*　　　*

The snow is deep, the new coat of varnish dry, and I set out on a foray alone, a pilgrim in search of . . . what? What is it pilgrims seek, and do they ever find it? As I scuff through the woods on this snowy evening my mind focuses on the start of the new year. It is a time for resolve and resolution, for reconfirming commitments. Heaven only knows I have no scarcity of resolutions to make, were I willing to do so. I could certainly be more patient with the children, less inclined to raise my voice. I would serve myself well not to smoke cigarettes any more. I could try harder to perceive my wife not through the filter of my expectations, but on the terms of her realities. I really ought to organize my time more willfully so as to produce more; the new book is going altogether too slowly.

I am only subliminally aware of my surroundings along the familiar trail. A dark blob in a skeletal tamarack is a sleeping partridge; another blob on a nearby popple is a cluster of leaves that have defied the stripping winds — I had noticed it on an earlier walk. The soft, silent glide of an owl is swallowed by the soundless night, and the faint light of half moon combines with the snow to indicate the path. Animal tracks are emphasized by shadow, made indistinct again by sifting snow. I don't stop to examine, engrossed by my inward journeys to the exclusion of outer reality, satisfied to be aware that some things — rabbits, foxes, squirrels — have been here.

That damned squeak again. It is too faint to offend nearby wildlife, but *I* know it is there like a confounded tinnitus whistling in my ear. The other snowshoe answers *scuff-scuff*, a concert breaking in on my introspection. How can I be introspective, philosophical, contemplative, with that annoyance at my feet?

I am nearing the river, winding through the willows of the marsh and closing on the landmark birches that line the bank. The open water is black, sibilant; occasional ice chunks loosen from the four-foot-wide lining along the riverside and gurgle as they dive and bob downstream. I prop the snowshoes against the trunk of the big birch where I have a favorite roost and use them for a backrest, the tails stuck in the snow.

Watching the coursing water, my mind cascades over the unlimited subject of appropriate resolution material, but it is unable to fasten on a good, workable topic, though I have several to suggest to various members of my family, friends, and associates. Perhaps I should pick on something simple, small, and finite. Something I could surely accomplish and thereby save myself the inevitable denigration of too lofty an aspiration, which invites noncompliance, followed by remorse and reconfirmation of my failings. I have it: I will fix those snowshoes once and for all. But no, that's been tried and has failed each time. Maybe those snowshoes are *meant* to squeak and scuff. But why? Human failings are usually by human design and intent, however subconscious. If so, why do I want those snowshoes to make noise? The sound disturbs my maunderings and compels me to attend to the here and now.

That's it, of course. Life is not a promissory note, or rumination on the past — life is now, this moment, the instant something occurs. And I know now what my resolution shall be.

I will wear metaphorical snowshoes to bring me in closer contact with the here and now more often. That way I will be able to listen to Tony when he bursts through the door, fresh from the school bus and bubbling with news from school, instead of asking him to wait until I have convenience and patience; we will have a natural communion and enjoyment of the moment, instead of frustration for him and condescension for me when I ask later, if I even think of it: "And what happened in school today?" That way I can respond when David wants to share a piece of artwork with me, when others are willing to let their lives touch mine.

I resolve to be like Frank DeClusin of long ago, putting on my snowshoes literally and allegorically, to visit my friends when I am lonely, and to let my lives be touched by theirs, and to make the effort of the long walk that is sometimes required.

I rise, buckle on my snowshoes, and go through woods "lovely, dark and deep, but I have promises to keep, and miles to go before I sleep."

7 The Snail That Played Downhill Racer

Walking through woods in early winter was easy and full of delights and greetings as wildlife left spoors on the thin cover of snow. Whole epochs were written there of high drama and adventure in the lives of fox, partridge, rabbits, and many kinds of rodents. Even squirrels left telltale flakes from pine cones chewed far up in the trees. Now the snow is deep, and while the life sagas are still scribed in it, moving about has become harder for bipeds, as for deer, and snowshoes are a slow mode of travel.

A confirmed downhill skier, I have looked longingly at the television commercial showing a cross-country ski champion. He seems to float across the snow, a ballet dancer with one leg and one ski in the air, the other zooming over the white blanket as though it were gossamer. Then he alternates. He doesn't ski, never exerts himself, but speeds through the snow, uphill and down, a Peter Pan of the winter woods. That's the way to go!

The family is divided. Tony relishes speed. Skis connote Downhill Racer, slaloms, sprays of powder snow at sixty miles an hour. He has never done any of these, but in his mind's eye he always fancies speed.

"Cross-country skis?" Tony says dubiously. "Aren't they sort of, well, you know, slow?"

David is somewhere on the scale between noncommittal and mildly interested: "I suppose."

"Absurd!" says Peggy. Years ago, when we courted, I took her skiing. It was a fiasco that came close to rupturing our budding romance. The slope was icy, Peggy had never been on skis and was nervous. The tow had taken us atop the intermediate hill. I was experienced and had extreme difficulty with the steeply sloping icefield; Peggy arrived at the bottom bruised, vowing never to repeat the experience.

"I mean cross-country skis, not downhill," I explain.

"That's different. Yes, I think that might be fun."

*   *   *

It's so easy! Why haven't we done this long ago! The skinny cross-country skis, unlike my old downhill ones, glide across uneven terrain, and it *is* fun to go scudding along. They are slower on the downhill runs, but it is much easier going uphill. Much more effortless, faster, than snowshoes. But when everything is said and done, I am no butterfly dancing across the snow; I am still an earthling, a groundbound biped.

Over my shoulder I see someone thrashing on the ground, a tangle of skis and poles.

"Get yourself sideways to the hill," I yell, "or you'll slide downhill as you get up."

The advice comes too late and Tony is furious as he extricates himself from another tangle and cascade of snow. Tony always wants instant success and perfection from himself; David, from others.

Peggy and David are coming along now, snowplowing as though their lives depended on it, though the terrain slopes very gently. It's not even a hill, just the whisper of an incline. They have their brakes on and come to a stop before the bottom.

"Isn't this fun?" I demand.

Everyone agrees, but there is an aura of caution, of recalcitrance to the admission.

*   *   *

Early Sunday morning I set out with the brush hook in one hand, both ski poles in the other, intent on carving out a trail. David wants to come along, then Tony joins us, and the three of us plod along. Across the ice of the little lake, up into the pine plantation. The frozen branches lop off easily, making a handsome opening among the Norways.

"Doesn't that hurt the trees?" David asks.

"Not if you cut clean along the trunk. Norway pines can be pruned up to two-thirds of their height."

There is a brisk wind belying the relatively balmy temperature somewhere in the teens. Doing the brushing warms me, though, and the boys while away the slack time going back and forth on the trail behind me, packing the soft snow.

"Greasing it," Tony explains. "It goes faster."

Through the tall pines of the natural wood stand, back into the plantation. Then we are at the breakaway where the higher ground falls off to the marsh. It is a lovely little hill, and we go back and forth, skiing down and plodding back up, until even Tony is satisfied with the rate of acceleration.

*   *   *

Bergstroms come in the afternoon, bringing their skis. Carol and some of their offspring have participated in cross-country ski races in past years. We file down the path and the realization dawns on me that Tony and David have somehow become comfortable on their skis. It is important to learn that there are many ways to move through life, not just the automobile and television. One can walk, ski, snowshoe, run, sampling much more than if one hurried through a windshield tour of life or glued one's mind to the tube. One can have friends, have dialogue and conversation, share feelings, activities, and care. I do not tell Tony and David this, it is after all my own abstraction, and all that I can really do is to provide the experiences for them and hope they will retain what is of value to them.

The new ski trail is a pleasure; it is my first outing on it, unencumbered by brush hook, and I can just enjoy scudding, gliding, feeling greater ease and less work as my stride lengthens and I have to take fewer steps.

On the hilltop among the huge old Norway pines, Peggy and I find ourselves side by side, a little winded from the uphill climb, very warm despite the brisk wind against our cheeks. I've not bothered Peggy with advice and admonitions, and now she is over the trepidation and nervousness just by virtue of easing into the cross-country skiing.

"This is beautiful," she says, and starts on the curving down-hill slide, knees bent, elbows in, floating amid the trees.

We meet again at the bottom, having coasted to a stop on the upgrade among the pine trees we have planted, where the trail curves and continues out of sight.

"Full moon tonight. Shall we come out after the children are asleep?"

*   *   *

A brittle night cast in silvery blues, blacks, and utter white. We coast, skim through the world of trees and silence, accustomed now to the soft sliding motion. I will always be earthling, forever a skier unable to dance ballet on the slim boards, but forever grateful for the opportunity to enjoy the northwoods on limited skill but an unlimited capacity for appreciation.

8 Who Owns My Land?

The letter seemed innocuous, worded in bureaucratic hedgings, but the import was ominous. They did not own their homestead, their land, where the family had lived for three generations. Maybe. Perhaps. It remains to be seen.

"It's a mistake?" Fran is wishful but nervous. "Great-grampa bought it as tax forfeited. That's what Dad said."

"This letter doesn't make sense," Carl complains, rereading it.

They fetch the tattered abstracts and title papers from the fish tackle box containing family documents. The land had been acquired by Fran's great-grandfather at a tax forfeit sale conducted by the state in 1911. The title was clear. There were the usual mortgages and loans, some liens during the depression years, and late payment of taxes; but all had been satisfied long ago, long before title had come to Fran when her father's estate was probated.

"I don't understand it," she says.

"Maybe I should call the man at the Bureau of Indian Affairs who sent it," Carl suggests. "Maybe it's a mistake."

* * *

A few miles down the road the confusion is just as great.

"Hey, it says here that maybe we own that eighty acres up the road where Fran and Carl live!" Don is incredulous and Shirley crowds, leaning over his shoulder to read the letter.

"BIA says we are the heirs, that the land was an allotment to my grandmother. . . . No, that couldn't be. Great-grandmother? Great-great? I'll have to find out."

"It doesn't say *you* are the heir," Shirley points out. "It says *one of the heirs*. And it says you *may* be. It's just more pie in the sky. Promises."

Shirley says "promises" with contempt. It is a dirty word.

"The old folks always said there was some land up that way belonged to the family." Don is forever the optimist. "Let's find out!"

*　　　　*　　　　*

At the Bureau of Indian Affairs field office the phones are ringing with inquiries out of all proportion to the number of land parcels involved. About thirty property owners had been notified in the first mailing that their titles might be invalid, although many more such notices are in process. The agency's superintendent is bemused, a bit harassed, burdened by the knowledge that more, many more notices could ultimately be issued.

It had begun inauspiciously two years before, when the bureau belatedly, with much prodding, assigned summer help consisting of college students the task of checking old land records to insure no claims for damages could ever arise. Congress had passed a statute of limitations some years before, seeking to put an end to Indian land claims that had to be handled by the government. The law required the bureau to dragnet possible claims in an all-out, final effort. The expectation was that not much more would be found; Indian claims had been pursued, off and on, for so long that it would be surprising to unearth new discoveries. The government wanted to be quit of the claims business, leaving it to individuals to go to the civil courts.

Fran and Carl are ushered into the superintendent's office, seeking an explanation.

"It seems that your great-grandfather bought a former Indian allotment at a tax forfeiture sale," the superintendent explains.

"We know about the sale," Carl says. "It's in the title papers. What's an allotment?"

"Back in the late 1890s and early 1900s the government divided many Indian reservations among the people living there. Each person received a parcel of land, and the surplus was sold. What the individual received was called an allotment, and your land was one."

"If the Indian who owned it didn't pay his taxes, and it was sold, why should we worry about it today?" Carl is defensive, angry.

The superintendent is uncomfortable, but wades right in: "The land was not subject to state and local taxes. It was still held in trust by the federal government for the Indian, so he was right in not paying his taxes. The mistake was in imposing the taxes and then in selling the land as forfeited. . . ."

"They didn't have a right to sell it to my great-grandfather?" Fran is shocked. "Whose fault is that?"

"The state and the county. And the federal government; we should have caught it when it happened."

"And we may lose our land today because you slipped up seventy years ago?" Carl is flushed, veins standing out on his forehead. "I mean, not you personally, but your office. And the state." He tries to make amends.

"That's entirely possible, and you should think about getting a lawyer," the superintendent advises.

As he answers the questions he knows there will be many more such meetings. The summer students had opened Pandora's box, finding whole categories of irregularities: rights of way had been granted to railroads, for highways, to power companies, without Indian-owner permission—damages could be due. Where rights of way were no longer used, ownership should have reverted to the original Indian titleholder, but instead the land was sold. Such sales could be invalid, if made without the knowledge and consent of the owner. In another instance, a large block of land including Indian allotments was set aside as a wildlife refuge by the federal government, apparently without ever asking or offering to reimburse the Indian owners—and a sizable court case could be triggered by that. All told, many thousands of acres could be involved just in northern Minnesota; hundreds of thousands of acres could be at stake across the nation.

"I told you not to believe it!" says Shirley.

"I didn't say you would not get the land," the superintendent repeats, "or damages or reimbursement. What I said was that you are *one* out of sixty-four heirs to that eighty acres, and each and every one of the sixty-four has to be found and has to agree on what you want to do with this matter. So far we have located forty-nine, and we are still looking for the other fifteen."

Some parcels have hundreds of heirs, each owning a fraction; the heirs are scattered from coast to coast, not aware they may have rights to land that was thought to have been lost long ago.

*   *   *

At a public meeting realtors express their dismay; buyers are wary, unsure the titles are valid. A county attorney suggests that Congress ought to pass a law reimbursing Indian heirs, but some tribal leaders are of the opinion that if the land rightfully belongs to Indian heirs of long-ago allottees, the land should be returned, even if each instance has to be heard in the courts.

"I don't even know if I should put in the garden this year," says Fran as they leave the meeting hall. Like her parents, Fran and Carl have a large garden, raise some livestock, but depend on Carl's job in town.

"I guess we get a lawyer and put in the garden," says Carl. Whatever the sins of long ago, it was their land now and they would hold on to it.

*   *   *

"You'd better stay on that construction job," Shirley tells Don. "Nothing will come of this, you'll see." She hopes something will, but does not want to say so and jinx their luck.

"Couldn't afford to quit even if we got the land back. But I will get a lawyer," Don agrees.

Neither says it, both think it: This was how so much Indian land was stolen, taken away; it's our responsibility to get it back if we can. No, not get it back—by rights it is still Indian land. Regain possession.

*   *   *

In Minnesota an estimated 150,000 to 250,000 acres could be subject to potential lawsuit to determine rightful ownership. In the Dakotas, Montana, and elsewhere even more land could be involved. No legislation can eliminate the right of the owners or their heirs to sue to clear title. Now or twenty years from now. Or a hundred years from now.

9 Nearer, My Washington, to Thee

It is the time of year for the annual township meetings. We will emerge from our northwoods sanctuaries, our little farms, hideaways, and the growing number of just plain residences as suburban sprawl punctuates what used to be pristine woods. We will congregate in our clapboard town halls. The parking areas will have been plowed, cobwebs blown out of antediluvian heating units, dust wiped off the benches.

Friends and neighbors will gather, vowing to see more of each other and wondering why there isn't time to get together for whist as we used to in the days before television. Folks will be friendly, accommodating the new faces, secretly wondering whence all these new people are coming; they are not all that different, these newcomers—a teacher, a telephone company employee, a retired military person—it's just that there are more of them. More people willing to surrender the graces, culture, and comforts of the corporate limits for the privacy of the countryside, the very numbers defeating the purpose.

The agenda will include perennial topics. Some township roads and bridges need work, but there is no money. The township zoning ordinance requiring a minimum of five acres per subdivided lot is under assault, besmirched by the grandfathered smaller lots some developers carved out before the ordinance was passed. The coffee urn is due to expire any moment, same as last year.

*   *   *

A week before the annual meeting the Township Zoning

Board convenes at a regular session. The county commissioner drops in. It appears something different will enter the equation at next week's annual meeting.

A new agenda has crept in over the years. Newer even than the growing demand for more town roads to serve the growing population, more snowplowing, maintenance, and services.

The upper Mississippi runs through the township. There is a move afoot, and has been since the Wild and Scenic Rivers Bill was passed by Congress in 1968, to so designate the river. This would lead to sections set aside for wildlife, others for scenic value, others yet for recreation, and a few perhaps left out of the plan since they are too built-up to warrant inclusion. Our congressman has been fighting it, delaying the process of designation with demands for a park service master plan before allowing the matter to be considered again. Meanwhile a state senator has come up with a proposal that the eight counties involved set up a consortium to manage the river, preempting the federal effort. How do we feel about it? Would we go to a public meeting to be conducted soon by the feds to declare ourselves? Discuss it at the annual meeting? The county commissioner reports on all this, gingerly feeling out sentiment.

"I don't want some idiotic bureaucrat telling us what to do," someone around the table says. It's good for a laugh. Jibes at the federal government are always good for a laugh; it's so far away. Shots at the state government are good for a chuckle. The county commissioners are taboo, since their financial aid has direct bearing on township roadwork.

"Who will pay for maintenance and upkeep, and services, of the multicounty river system?"

"There won't be any," the commissioner says. "It would just be a cooperative zoning effort."

So the preemptive plan would not achieve the same purposes of preservation, protection, furnishing of services and reclamation, as would the park service Wild and Scenic Rivers plan. Nor would there be any means of acquiring land to be put in the public domain for access, camping, and other uses. Would it even halt or slow riverbank real estate development? The inexorable, mushrooming pollution?

"There's another item," the commissioner says, hoping it will be added to the annual meeting agenda: Since the 1930s the old Harold Ickes proposal for a "palms to pines" road system has been kicking around. The notion is to enable motorists to drive from New Orleans to Lake Itasca with side trips to pretty places. When first proposed it was a good WPA project, would have aided commerce and agriculture; the highways of the 1930s were a far cry from what they are today. Now there are plenty of farm-to-market roads to most places, and the idea of a superhighway so gas-guzzlers can zoom the length of the Mississippi should bring joy only to the hearts and pocketbooks of OPEC, Arab sheiks, and the oil companies.

The questioning becomes sharp, the commissioner becomes defensive.

"Nobody wants new roads," the commissioner explains. "This is just a way for the county to get financial aid we couldn't otherwise get to make road improvements we'd have to make anyway."

There is silence. The pocketbook has been reached, wrung, wrenched. We'll have to pay for fixing that road anyhow; why not use the Great River Road money so tantalizingly tossed our way and save ourselves some bucks? Why not spread the cost among 200 million taxpayers to help pay what otherwise a few thousand of us would have to finance? State highway money might be a few decades away. It is tempting though we all know the arguments against enhancing automobile travel.

"About how much Great River Road money would be available in the county? In the township?"

Nobody knows, but the educated guesses are in the range of several million dollars. Again there is silence, a mental patting of wallets and checkbooks.

"That much money would be a good start to get us passenger rail service again!" It used to be our lifeline, now reduced to freight service.

"I'm all for getting back passenger train service," the commissioner assures. "But this River Road money is available now, and we have to move on it if we want it."

"Are these two, the Wild and Scenic River designation and the Great River Road, coordinated?" a questioner speaks up. "Or are we going to build a road where some time later there is going to be wilderness?"

"They are not coordinated. There is no coordination between those two, or the eight-county plan," the commissioner says. "None of those feds work together."

But isn't the county board, which must act on all these things, a point of coordination? Aren't we, in township meeting, a point of coordination? Even if the feds and the state officials in various departments are not?

"Those bureaucrats sure don't know what they are doing," someone says. "Wasting all that money, trying to tell us what to do. But we sure could stand the help fixing up the old road. . . ."

*   *   *

And there you have it. Washington is "them," absurd wastrels whose geriatric budget cycles regurgitate ancient projects to be paid with tomorrow's taxes. And we "just plain folks" are "smart," enthusiastically spending money thus available, denouncing our very selves for making it available—for the "them" is really "we."

The truth is that the road is not even in need of repairs, and will not be for many years to come. The new spur roads that will radiate from it, accruing benefit only to real estate speculators, may have to be torn out when the Wild and Scenic River designation comes about.

Could it be that the wasteful idiots who don't know what they are doing are not only in Washington, but also at our own annual town meeting?

10 Spring's Reminder for the Caretaker

The clear roads give the lie to the true state of things.

Occasional signs, put up temporarily by the highway department during the spring breakup, limit the weight per axle of vehicles. Heavy logging trucks and other big equipment are unable to use many roads and bridges during those few weeks, usually a month. As the ground thaws and the retreating frost expands and contracts and heaves, the heavy traffic would damage the roadbed and surface.

Cars, pickup trucks, vans, and the like have no trouble. The roads are clean and clear, bordered by receding snowbanks that had piled up, drifted, been plowed aside, during the winter. One is free to drive to town, to drive anywhere really on paved roads and improved gravel, thinking that winter has departed. But that is an illusion because in the real world of the woods this can be the most inhospitable of times.

*   *   *

Before the advent of improved roads and heavy equipment to build and clear them, spring breakup meant isolation and sometimes being cooped up in your shelter for a considerable time. The lake and river ice was no longer safe to travel: an end to families pulling their toboggans, journeying many miles to visit friends, to trap, to hunt.

An old Indian man once told me, looking out over the frozen panorama of Leech Lake on a winter's day: "It looks so sad, so empty. When I was young I could always see people out there, going visiting. Now there is no one and the ice is empty."

Yet even in the old days when Indian moieties ranged from the small winter camps of dispersed families to the larger summer villages, spring breakup was a time for staying home, hoping for a sufficient food supply, and preparing for sugar time that was soon to follow as the days warmed and the nights cooled, and the sap coursed up and down the trunks of the maples.

The journals, accounts, and recollections of *fin de siècle* homesteaders and loggers also reflect the cabin fever, the feeling of imprisonment, engendered by spring breakup. It was a time when corduroy roads heaved, when one step was on frozen ground and the next step in a pool of deep muck. It was a time to stay put and to hope that the thaw would be brief.

*   *   *

I am impatient to be out in the woods, to roam the familiar places, to soak up the warmth and the odors of nascent spring. It is too early for even the earliest of wildflowers, and an exercise of the imagination to see the swelling of buds. But the bright sun and the stirrings of anticipation, if not of fact, are enough to propel me to the forest.

Here and there sere grass appears through the snow. Evaporation, more than outright melting, is shrinking the white blankets. Trees and landmarks seem to grow tall overnight, while it is only the ground-covering snow that is compacting, lengthening the visible portions of the trunks. I follow one of the cross-country ski trails and find branches that brushed my face a few weeks ago above my head.

The crusty, crystalline snow surface is so uneven that skiing is impractical. The thickness of the crust is irregular, beneath there are air pockets, more crystallized snow, and none of the stuff that made for gliding through the winter woods. I think back longingly on the moments when, warmed and loosened, skiing through the woods was the living of a fairy tale — soundless magic motion. Now the smallest movement is accompanied by loud crunching.

Snowshoes, too, fail to serve their purpose, and I leave my

scarred familiars hanging on the wall. So strong is the urge to visit a favorite hillside that I set out on foot.

I walk gingerly, hoping to sneak across the crust, stepping lightly into that good day. When my hopes are up after three successful steps, the fourth footfall breaks through and I am in snow to my knees. Pull up the foot, set it down softly, break through again. It is very hard walking. Expecting to break through on the succeeding step, I find firm crust instead and rise above the entrapment. The next step finds me breaking through again.

This is too much, I think, too hard to make it worthwhile. But now I am as far from the house as from the hilltop. Out of breath, perspiring, out of sorts, I arrive at my destination. I sit on a fallen log, listening to my respiration rate subside. The towering pines behind me, the still-frozen lake in front, I am for once not touched by the visual beauty. I am still too hot, too out of breath, miffed that it should be so hard to visit a favorite lookout.

Around and about, fluttering near my head, chickadees welcome me. But they also fail to cheer; I wish for juncos and robins, for the sound of a sparrow's song. Even the ravens have not yet given way to the crows, and the first migrating hawk has yet to appear.

How can it be that a place so familiar at all other times of the year should be so difficult to reach? That my beloved land should be so inhospitable to its caretaker-custodian? This does not feel right. I own this place and treat it with respect; why can't it reciprocate? I have abstract and title, all documents properly recorded by the Register of Deeds. You can't do this to me, beloved acres! Do I have to stand atop this hill and wave ownership papers at you to prove my point? Where is your gratitude for my debarring motorcyclists and snowmobiles that were speeding the erosion of the hillside? Your thanks for my picking up the continuously accumulating debris thrown from passing cars, the cans, candy wrappers, and assorted junk? Your appreciation for my planting of caragana to feed the birds and hold the embankment, for underplanting trees and juniper? For that secret seedbed of blueberry plants, for my not telling *any-*

one about the rare wild orchids at the foot of the hill?

*   *   *

Breakup compels me to accept that official records notwith-standing, I can not own the land. I may enjoy limited privileges of use and caring tenancy, but mortal humans can not be the proprietor of immortal creation. I can share and participate, try to tend this patch, but my pilgrimage is a rite of passage; I did not create this place, I can not control it.

That I can not course my property at breakup time is perhaps a necessary reminder of the limitations of human proprietor-ship.

A small, brilliant flash draws me out of reverie and I squint across the painfully blinding brightness of the snow, upward to the blue sky, avoiding the overhead sun. Then I see the coast-ing, swooping form. It is black against the blue, save for the iridescent head and tail. The first bald eagle has returned.

Both of us are on a sojourn. His betokens grace and goodness in relationship to creation; does mine?

11 Moments of Madness

It does not matter whether one lives in the middle of a big city or in the northwoods. There are occasions, moments, instances of insanity in life, and I try to get through them as best I can. *Long* afterwards, I can force a smile.

When the twins were six months old and we were living in a big city, my wife had to go on an out-of-town business trip. She had been gone only a few hours when everything came apart at the seams. The two older boys were having a loud, raucous dispute that echoed through the house; the twins were tired, hungry, and due for baths, each squalling and neither amenable to comforting. I felt harassed, sure one of my editors would call momentarily, reminding me of an overdue manuscript, and trying to cope with the here-and-now by doing one thing at a time. I am not very graceful or calm.

"Tony and David!" I yell. "Stop that fighting or else!"

But I am impotent with one baby over the sink, the other screaming, and the older boys spatting, certain in the knowledge that I can do nothing.

Doorbell and telephone sound simultaneously.

"Come in," I say into the phone, hanging up, and, "I'll talk to you later," to the modishly dressed young man at the door; he comes in looking perplexed. I see his lips moving but the decibel level is such that I cannot hear what he is saying.

"Sit down while I get these babies settled," I shout at him.

Megan's face is purple with rage, Micah is screaming his lungs out. Tony and David have escalated hostilities upstairs, it sounds like World War Three. The young man sits down, his pale face is pasty, and he is rigid in the straightbacked chair, the nearest seating to the door.

A few minutes pass as I get Megan into pajamas and bed and hold Micah over the sink. In the momentary lull I notice that the stranger's face is chalky, beads of perspiration are standing on his forehead, running into his eyes, he looks on the brink of panic.

"When is Felice coming downstairs?" he whispers.

There is no Felice in our household. He is at the wrong house. Felice lives next door, a lissome twenty-year-old. Apparently he had come to pick her up on a date, arriving at the wrong house.

"She lives next door," I explain. But he has gone, bolting before I can say more.

Next day I apologize to Felice and try to explain to *her*, and she smiles wanly. "It was the strangest date I ever had. He thought those were my children and I hadn't told him about them."

*   *   *

Spring breakup is not my best time. The winter has been long, the last few weeks not conducive to outdoors fun. The driveway is impassable, a quagmire avoided even by dog and cat, although Tony and David seem to think that all the mud is a welcome change; their clothes and the entryway reflect it. I want everyone to cater to my whims, wishes, and needs as I construe them; but the rest of the family has identical notions, which I am reluctant to acknowledge.

"I have a case in district court first thing this morning," Peggy disappears through the door, splendidly dressed, shining briefcase in hand. I don't believe there is a case, and for all I know there is no district court within a thousand miles; she just wants to escape. Outside the door she says something about the driveway, I can't quite make out the words as she starts on the long walk to the road where the car is parked.

Through the kitchen window I see our black and white cat, tail high in the air, fur puffed up. What is he excited about? It is not the cat; it is a neighborhood skunk who festoons our front yard, feasting on food scraps that Tony and David insist on leaving.

"Dear God!" I pray. "Not today! Please send the dog a mile east and the cat a mile west! Just for a few minutes. Please."

It is not your customary prayer. Neither dog nor cat have learned that chasing this skunk is a losing proposition.

The phone rings. The baby sitter can't get her car started, and she is sick, and would I mind terribly if she didn't make it to work today. I mind but by then she has hung up. Today of all days! The older boys are home from school. Mud vacation. I start a new prayer asking divinity to eliminate mud vacations.

Tony is in the doorway dripping mud from the waist down, his rubber boots caked. As I inhale, preparatory to a scolding, he announces: "The creek is open and running. . . ."

". . . but not through the culvert!" David finishes for him. He, too, is in the kitchen, cascading mud.

"It washed out *under* the culvert. Will the fish be able to come up the creek under the culvert?"

Prospects of the roadway collapsing. Then it happens. The twins commence a tug of war with the knitting, dog and cat get into it with each other this time, I can hear the ruckus and glimpse the combat through the window. The phone rings and there is a knock on the door. It is one of those times.

"I don't want any," I say into the phone; to the opening door I pronounce, "I know that story is overdue but I put it in the mailbox this morning." An outright lie.

"I am your census taker," the lady at the door explains. "May I come in?"

She is muddy to her shins and trying to be polite.

*　　　*　　　*

I am a good host, offer coffee and courtesy, but it is difficult. Tony and David are hovering, still wearing muddy boots in the house and I want very much to abuse, to batter them, but that isn't done in front of company, especially a Representative of the Government. Micah has opened the flour bin and Megan is dishing it out. I plunge to stop them, spilling coffee.

Back at the table, watching for the next disaster, I tell the census taker that I mailed the form, all filled out. I hope this will truncate the interview, and am ready to plead that the television ads said to mail the forms, while the radio ads said to hold on to them.

"But you weren't supposed to," she is petulant, fishing out a new form from the sea of papers spread on the kitchen table, trying to keep the twins' hands off the file folders.

"Isn't that the form stuck on the calendar?" David is being helpful.

We go through the form line by agonizing line. I am questioned, challenged, interrogated.

"You put down 'Indian', but that boy and that girl don't look very Indian."

"Well, they are. My wife is Indian."

Tony looks *very* Indian, twin Micah so-so, twin Megan is blond and blue-eyed, David has red hair and brown eyes. The census taker is dubious.

"Do you want to see us dance?" David asks.

"No, not now!" I yell but it is too late as David and Tony oblige with their best Indian dancing and the twins join in.

"Change mine," I grit through my teeth, "to Druid." I am thinking of human sacrifices.

* * *

It ends as all such times must. The census lady leaves, the twins go to bed, Tony and David declare a truce, the baby sitter phones to say she has been able to start the car and has made a marvelous recovery and will be out some time later. My train of thought recedes from the homicidal to manslaughter or less. Another knock on the door.

"Your driveway is kind of bad," it is the census lady again.

"You didn't drive your car. . . . ?"

She had. The muffler floats halfway between the lilac and the willow. The car rests peacefully, its frame firmly in the mud, the wheels out of sight. I may have to amend my census form, listing one more resident in the special column for unexpected guests.

12 Battle of the Beavers

The engineers have come and gone, their parting words lingering in our ears long afterwards: "Building a bridge will cost ten, twenty thousand dollars. If it can be built. The peat depth would have to be tested to determine how far down the pilings have to be driven before meeting solid ground."

Pilings?

Pile-drivers on our tree farm?

Ten or twenty or more thousands of dollars because those furry things out there have to keep their teeth from growing too long?

And they are out there, under the ice, multiplying.

Any day now the lake will be open water and they will appear, paddling around, chewing trees, and building dams that will flood us out even more than last year. Because there will be more of them. Many more.

Within days I and mine will be under attack and we will be helpless because all attempts at introducing planned parenthood among *Castor canadensis* have failed. Perhaps our beavers are Catholics.

Their return two years ago was proof that wildlife conservation works, that a tree farm draws species long absent, that there was hope for the world. Now look at us, on the verge of being flooded out again, only more so.

There will be many more and heaven only knows which way they will scatter and what additional dams they will build. By last fall it was clear, all else having failed, that there was no choice but to curtail the beaver population. Not eradicate, but to cut it down somewhat. Steps were taken but they faltered.

49

*   *   *

"I'll come over and get rid of those beavers for you," my brother-in-law promises. He traps full time and while it is a considerable drive from his home to ours, he comes at the start of the season in December. A variety of traps and snares are dangling over his shoulder, and we set off through the woods to the lodges. The lakes are still open.

It is hard work to set and bait the traps, working in icy water near the slippery shore. He stakes conibear traps in the water passages, the channels scooped out by the beavers in readying for the winter ice. They will use the troughs to swim in and out of the lodge. Food caches that do not fit in the lodge are stored in the water nearby. The conibears are "humane" traps, painless, killing instantly, unlike the old-fashioned leg traps in which an animal, once caught, can suffer a long time. But the conibears don't work.

Our beavers push sticks into the trigger mechanism, setting off the traps, and then swim blithely on their way. The conflict becomes more intense, more personal, as Brother sets more conibears. All are sprung except one, in which a muskrat has been caught.

His reputation at stake, Brother sets and baits the traps ever more artfully, artistically, with ancient invocations, offerings, sprinkles of castor, bait of succulent popple, and trappers' tricks. But the beavers either swim around his offerings or spring the traps.

"Leg traps," he says. "That'll get them."

An adult beaver, weighing about fifty pounds, is caught in a leg trap at the dam during the night. Our dog investigates. The beaver lunges, gashes the dog on the forehead. In the process, the beaver frees itself from the trap, leaving three toenails behind. We now provide pedicures for beavers. The dog is taken to the veterinarian for stitches.

"It's too far to drive," Brother says.

*   *   *

A few hundred or thousand years ago, beavers hereabouts

grew to a much larger size: six, seven feet long, weighing hundreds of pounds. Just think what *those* beavers could have done to us! Perhaps I should count myself fortunate that ours are only two or three feet long and weigh, at most, sixty to seventy pounds.

"I'll get those beavers for you," a friend offers. "My partner and I run a trapline. We'll come out and get them in no time at all. You ever eat beaver? Delicious!"

I am skeptical about the delicious part. Everyone around is forever touting the succulence of wild game, such as porcupine, and bristles with recipes, but not a one of them has ever eaten a porky and all of them hedge when I offer to furnish one. However, I promise the family beaver for Christmas in lieu of goose. Cheaper, rich in protein, and a constructive use of the meat. It is in part a gesture to the arch-conservationist children.

Tony is not impressed.

"There goes my supply of antique bottles," sneers David.

"Food, good, good," says Micah, who treasures anything edible.

Megan and Peggy take a wait-and-see attitude.

The partners come and set traps. The lake is frozen now and they must chop through the ice to place the traps, and each day thereafter as the ice forms overnight, in order to check the traps. These trappers have tricks of which Brother hasn't dreamed. They too have invocations, offerings, baits, and contraptions. One masterpiece of trappers' craft consists of a long popple pole (delicious beaver food), with boards fastened at the bottom end, and four traps chained to the boards. But the beavers once again send a hapless muskrat to spring one trap, use sticks to trigger the rest. The sticks are left behind; they are thumbing their noses (teeth?) at us.

Car trouble, domestic demands, and other unexplained difficulties force the partners to surrender my territory. The beavers are safe once again, the trappers are gone, and I begin to wonder what will happen in the spring. Game warden, trappers, and basic arithmetic indicate that the original four beavers now number between twelve and twenty; by spring the population will be between twenty and thirty. I look at the old dams,

the water level now frozen inches below the top of my driveway, and shudder.

*   *   *

Another pair of trappers comes to my rescue. They look the
part: bearded, grimy, uncommunicative about their arcane
craft. Dog watches from a careful distance; he hates going to
the vet. I keep away, hoping the trappers will do better without
my curiosity. But it looks as though they are going through the
same antics as my brother-in-law and the others.

Something new is added: One of the trappers falls into the
hole he has chopped in the ice. Is a beaver pulling him down by
the pantsleg? The ankle? No. Just gravity and the weight of his
winter clothes.

"We need some different traps; we'll be back," the trappers
say.

But they do not return.

*   *   *

It is warmer now, soon the ice will melt. The vapor plumes
from the top of the beaver lodges look twice as thick, three
times as hot, as earlier in the winter. Beaver midwives must be
busy. Last night I dreamt that giant prehistoric beavers seven
feet long were having a picnic on my front porch. They were
eating porch pillars, having swum to my doorstep.

13 The Swimming Hole That Polluted a Pond

We all want it better for our kids than it was for us, and wish to bestow to them as realities the substance of our dreams. I want my children to have a swimming hole. Close to the house, deep enough to dive and swim, shallow so they would not drown, private for fun and games, and public for me to see what was going on.

"They love to swim but we can't let them in the lake," my wife announces again.

We call our pond "the Lake." It is ringed by silt and peat, which act like quicksand. It is thirty feet deep in the middle. The rule in the family is that adults who are good swimmers don't go alone; all others stay out. It is a dangerous place.

We have often talked of scooping out a swimming hole in the creek feeding the lake, a few feet from our doorstep. It would be in sandy soil, safe, a lot of fun.

"I'll do it," I promise.

*   *   *

It takes less than a day for a dragline to widen, deepen the channel. By nightfall the big machine, looking like a steam-shovel, has clanked away, leaving a swimming hole nearly four feet deep in the center, thirty feet across. At a cost of nearly $400 we have a dream come true, a swimming hole in the woods where a kid can strip clothes and plunge into the water on the spur of the moment. We stand on the edge and gloat as Tony and David splash.

"Water's kind of brown," Tony says, not seeming to mind.

"That's from the peat when the dragline scooped it up and the water ran out of it. It's full of tiny particles of peat. Some of the peat got mixed with the water."

"Will it go away?"

"Oh yes, that will settle or wash downstream in a hurry."

"I'm standing on a spring!" David yells. "It's cold!"

An exposed vein of clay emits icy groundwater, which mixes slowly with the sunwarmed surface water.

"Gotcha!" David splashes Tony and we retreat.

*   *   *

A few days go by before the peaty discoloration disappears, though when the children play they stir up some of the bottom sediment, which is slow to resettle. Most of it washes downstream and is absorbed in the lake.

In late summer, the lake shows algae and weeds. "It must be the peat, acts as a fertilizer," we conclude unhappily. We call the county agent and the Department of Natural Resources, where our fears are confirmed.

"Peat consists of partially decomposed organic matter," they explain. "Leaves, stalks, branches. It acts like a fertilizer that releases nutrients very slowly."

That's not all. In winter as it decomposes, the organic matter consumes oxygen, taking it out of the water, leaving less for fish and other aquatic life. It's been a well-kept family secret that the little lake contains fish; when people inquire, we obfuscate.

"That little pothole have fish?" We laugh. They laugh. And go away. Then I fish. You can't tell that the lake is deep.

What will happen to fish, dependent on oxygen, when the lake freezes over in winter? Will our swimming hole project seventy feet upstream, impact on the ecological balance, and affect the fish population?

In spring as the ice begins to rot, dead fish come to the surface, and returning bald eagles perch on the receding ice pan, gorging themselves. By summer we accept that, indeed, the fish population has diminished. We had not meant to harm the environment in scooping out a swimming hole for the children, but it seems that we have done so.

Two years go by before a new ecological balance emerges. It seems the lake will have a larger measure of algae and growth on a permanent basis, though it will take a few more years before we can tell what will happen to the diminishing fish population. The swimming hole is fine, the lake is changed. In the creek, the exposed sand and clay allow the water to run off briskly, and the spring runoff is accelerated. In the lake the infusion of nutrients encourages waterplants and algae, like raw sewage dumped in a river or a lake. The lake is becoming eutrophic.

"I wish we could have burned the peat as fuel, or used it for fertilizer in the garden," my wife says wistfully. We still relish the swimming hole but are increasingly sensitive to its consequences.

We are coming to look about our region with new eyes, with a different perspective. Much of the north country is peatland, marsh. Millions of acres of it. A peat gasification project is being considered nearby. It would scoop up peat, mix it with water into a slurry like the black ooze that erupted from our swimming hole as we excavated it. The slurry would be piped to a nearby plant, squeezed dry, baked, and a synthetic gas manufactured. Over twenty years, about 200,000 acres would be mined, perhaps more.

Finland, Russia, some other countries extract chemicals from peat. Waxes, industrial lubricants, and other products emerge from this immature coal. One thousand acres of peat supplies several such factories for twenty years. Now our urgent need for new energy sources is causing us to consider revamping the landscape and environment, and if our tiny swimming hole is any indication, a 200,000-acre dredging could have monstrous and irrevocable results.

We look at the swimming hole, consider the new gasification plant, and wonder about the spring runoff and possible floods—for the peat sponges up much of the spring melt and releases it slowly. We wonder about brown water from the peatland watersheds finding its way into Red Lake or Voyageurs National Park, possibly affecting fishing; at Red Lake the Indians' fishing cooperative is one of the economic mainstays, and at Voyageurs and nearby, sport fishing is an essential ingredient of tourism. There could be impact on wildlife and on vegetation. And there is the possibility of adding to existing, increasing acid rain.

*   *   *

Tony and David beleaguer me. "Let's go swimming at Cass Lake!"

I've not said anything about the environmental impact of the swimming hole, not wanting to spoil their fun. But they seem to have drawn their own conclusions, and use of it has dwindled.

How sad that transliterating a dream into reality should go awry.

14 Spear Fishing

Some people stand in the icy waters of feeder creeks, if not in Lake Superior itself, to net smelt. The shiny, small fish congregate in wriggling, intertwined masses that gravitate to warmer water in spring. *Warm* is a relative term. Other people stand in the icy water of inland streams, fishing spears in hand, stabbing at the endless spawning runs of saugers, or suckers.

Like Roman gladiators, tridents and nets in hand, the brave souls are arrayed in waders or in shorts and tennis shoes. The variety of attire defies commonality or style. The denominator is a fierce avariciousness, a compulsion to spear as many fish as possible. The size of the take has no relationship to the spearer's capacity to eat, as witnessed by the many dead fish left behind at the end of each day, by the gratuitous offers of fish to friends and strangers, most of whom either have a surfeit of their own or detest what to others is a delicacy. Cleaning and smoking suckers is work.

*   *   *

"I want a fishing spear," David declares again; it has been a refrain since the arrival of spring when the lakes were still frozen.

"So do I," says Tony.

"All right, all right, I'll buy one," promises Peggy, and she buys one.

On the way to the spearing grounds the four of us debate who gets the first turn, who the second, and so on. It is inconclusive except that as I park the car I am the last to get out and automatically fourth with The Spear. David is in the river to his knees, oblivious to the cold, spear raised, poised, ready for the kill. Tony hops up and down the bank urging David to hurry and Peggy sits on a rock, informing both boys that her turn comes next and soon. I am not sure it is worth getting wet, cold, and skunked.

Dozens of people line the railing of the bridge over the Mississippi, watching suckers.

"Here comes a bunch now!" a bystander shouts. "No, no, next to you . . . they went right by you! Can't you see them? Right between your legs!"

The fishermen in the swift, cold current cannot tell to whom the gratuitous remarks are addressed and ignore them.

From the bridge the shapes of the tumultuous fish are clearly visible. Dark forms, some two feet long, racing, darting through the shallows, along the bottom rocks, impelled by the urgent need to disgorge spawn and to inseminate the spilled roe. For days now the northern pike have been coming upstream to perform the ritual, followed by walleye pike, both species rigorously protected during the spawning run. Now the saugers, a rough fish, are running and these may be speared, though not in the spawning grounds.

Somehow Tony has acquired the spear. "I got one, I got one," he yells, hoists the spear out of the water, and a two- to three-pound sucker is wriggling there, firmly impaled.

"I got one too!" shouts David. He has reached into the water with his bare hands and caught one. Other fisherman glare at David.

"Get out of here, kid," one mutters.

But David holds his ground, catches more barehanded, then uses a rock and stuns one. The family pile of fish on the bank is growing, though neither Peggy nor I have had a turn yet. The air is sunwarmed and clear, we are backdropped by pines and aspen along both shores as the seventy-foot-wide river curves downstream and away.

It is very beautiful and I tune in on the rippling of the water, the snatches of birdsong, the colors, and the clearness of the air; and I filter out the sounds of the spearers and their cheerleaders.

Upstream of the bridge, yellow and white signs announce that this is forbidden territory, sacred spawning grounds where the fish are to be left undisturbed. Statistically, few fish are speared, most run the gauntlet, spawn, and return downstream unscathed.

"Look what I found!" I don't even have to turn my head; if anything is found the discoverer is David. He holds a rusted fish spear in his hands, apparently lost by a fisherman long ago.

"It's pretty good," David says, balancing it. On inspection it turns out to be very old, forged and welded in someone's home workshop. Better than the one we purchased at the store. It is David's now, but my chance of spearing has suddenly gone from .250 to .333.

Peggy wades out, having somehow persuaded Tony to surrender the weapon.

"This I want to see," comes a voice from the bridge. It belongs to another attorney who has had professional contact with her, jousting in the local courts.

The family's *juris doctor* stands in the middle of the swirling Mississippi in tennis shoes, shorts, and ragged shirt wielding a fish spear. And she has the knack. A sucker is wriggling at the end of her spear. Then another. Is this what you learn in law school? Learned it as a kid, Peggy says while taking a break. She does not look smug but I know that she is feeling smug.

"Clarence Darrow spearing fish," I say over my shoulder, wading out to take my turn.

Standing in the water, the fish shapes look brown, almost invisible against the riverbottom. From the bridge they had looked black. My spear clangs against the rock and is retrieved, empty. I wince, thinking of having to straighten, sharpen bent spearpoints when we get home. Another lunge, another miss.

"What's wrong, Dad? Too slow?" Tony is solicitous and I pretend I don't know him, that he is speaking to someone else.

Then I connect, catch the rhythm of fish movements and avoidance patterns. I can't match Peggy's skill but at least I'm not a complete dunderhead.

On shore again, watching, I notice that some spearers heave their fish ashore where they plunk, splatter against the rocks to be picked up later. This bruises, damages the meat and seems to me a gesture of disrespect for wildlife and for food, a wastefulness. Contempt. Each of us had been caring enough to carry the catch ashore, or to hand it to a family member to be deposited. The callousness somehow dismays and offends me. It is not my value and view, and I am regretful that others are wanton.

Walking across the bridge to gaze upstream at the spawning grounds, filled with hundreds, perhaps thousands of fish, I see that three spearers have wandered into the forbidden grounds, spearing fish as they spawn. This is a violation not only of game laws, but also of the laws of life. The disruption of propagation is dreadful. Stemming from thoughtlessness, greed, it is the height of wastefulness, disrupting the spawning, and damaging deposited spawn with each footstep. The fish eggs need but a few days to hatch, the tiny spawn swimming away shortly after birth. Fish can be replenished, propagation can not.

At home we set up the cleaning table in the yard and proceed with the task. The cat hovers nearby, feigning disinterest; the dog approaches, sniffs, and departs. So does Tony, while Peggy must watch the twins (who are, I believe, sleeping). David and I fall to the cleaning chore.

The cleaned fish are frozen and stored until we can smoke them. Discarded fish parts go into the garden plot that a few weeks hence will be seeded to corn.

15 Spring Buds After a Hailstorm

"The darling buds of May" are fattening. Daily, hourly, the plants respond to the higher position of the sun, the intensification of light. Even the pine trees are tumescent with beginning growth, which in a few weeks will be pale green candles, the future trunks and branches.

We watch the growth, fascinated by the recurring miracle of photosynthesis and regeneration after dormancy. But there is an added element to the watchfulness.

During the winter we had sheared lower limbs among the Norway, or red, pine. This species can be limbed flush to the trunk nearly two-thirds of its height. The tree will do this by itself over a much longer timespan, the lower branches dying and eventually sloughing off. Our speeding this process produces more clear lumber (in two or three generations) and inhibits forest fires. Common spring grass fires sweeping through a plantation are denied the fuel of low branches; trees might scorch but are not as likely to burst into flames. There are no lower branches to carry a quick-burning grass fire into the crowns, where a true inferno could engender. While limbing trees we once again confront the damage of a storm a few years ago.

"Look at the scars," says Tony.

"Some of the branches break off," David adds, "where the scars are deep."

Branches and trunks are badly pitted. Huge hailstones driven by a hundred-mile-an-hour wind had blasted away bark and epidermis. Afterward, the wounds gathered pitch and began to grow over, but they are not yet entirely healed.

"We'll know in another two, three, maybe four years," I say.

Until the healing is complete we are not safe from insects and disease, threats normally warded off by healthy bark. Our plantation is, will be, vulnerable for some time to come.

When the storm hit, Peggy was away. Tony, David, and I were by ourselves and the twins had not yet been born.

*   *   *

Hot weather, sultry and oppressive. As day wears on the skies darken but there are no cloud formations; just a gradual, persistent leadening. The boys swim and play in the creek near the doorstep but have no gusto. It is too heavy.

We will get a good, stout summer storm, I think. I hope something will break the prolonged heat that has become overwhelming.

Tony and David eat without enthusiasm and for once go to bed of their own volition, tossing and turning before falling asleep. Ordinarily, when you are six and five, sleep comes easily after a busy summer day.

It should be daylight until well past nine at night in our northern latitude, but it gets progressively darker long before, windstill, with a heavy feel to the air. I examine the skies but see no roiling clouds that would cause worry about a fierce storm, and decide against turning on radio or television. We will get a good gullywasher, I think, checking on the now-sleeping children, then puttering about the yard to pick up the debris of toys, chairs, and clothes that are the residue of the day. Then I go indoors, try to concentrate on a book without success, and glance at the lake where movement has caught my eye.

There is a riffle of wind, then it is gone. Another, and it disappears as well. Still. Humid. Darkness of night now, long before it is due.

Rain and wind begin suddenly, an onslaught. It is violent and abrupt, joined quickly by drumming on the roof, on the west and north walls. Hail!

I leap out of the chair, rush to the door intending to close the shutters outside, but I am stopped at the threshold. Hailstones are bounding, cascading. Golf ball size, then tennis ball size.

They leap wildly about the yard, beginning to cover the ground, and I cannot exit the house without injury.

I open the door to the storm cellar, toss down the emergency supplies, then make another attempt to go outside to shutter the house. Rain slicker, gum boots, and hard hat. Even so I am driven back by the windwhipped ice balls coming almost horizontally. The wind is howling unlike any wind-sounds from the trees that I have ever heard before; it is swooshing, roaring, deafening amid the cacophony of the hailstones against the house.

It is machine-gun fire thudding all about me, bullets burying themselves in the earth and the trees. I mentally cower, time falling away until I am a dogface in a long-ago war and the live ammunition is pillowing all about me.

I *must* get outside and shutter the house before the windows are blown in! Or should I wake the boys, take them to the storm cellar, before making the attempt? Undecided. I try it outside and am driven back once again by the ice, the missiles horizontal. I go to the children's room to reassure and safeguard, and I find them cozy in the windowless northwest corner, still asleep, exhausted by play and weather, unaware of the ceaseless racket. If only I could shutter the north window in their room!

The roof leaks and the entire household array of pots, pans, and pails fails to catch the rain. They overflow; new leaks appear. Then a crash. Another. The windows are disintegrating under the merciless attack. In the living room. The kitchen. Then the boys' room. And still they sleep, amid pounding hailstones, roaring wind, and rain pouring into the house.

It stops after half an hour, forty-five minutes. I step outside into the cool and the calm, overwhelmed by the scent of pines.

One good thing, I think, is the smell of clean, fresh air, of evening cool and pine. There is nothing to be done now until the morrow. I mop as best I can, retrieve survival gear from the cellar.

The smell of pine is cloying now, a sickening sweetness, as I, too, go to sleep in the sodden mess of our home.

*   *   *

All about the ground are piles, mounds, of what had once been pine needles and the candle growths of the year. They have been minced into a pulp. What I had smelled as pine scent at first, and then as an overpowering aroma, had come from these mounds. There would be no growth of the pines at all this year, and the new stuff is strewn on the earth. It is in piles and in heaps beneath every single tree, young and old alike.

And then I see the naked wounds on the branches and the bare spots on the trunks. My eyes register the injuries, the damage; my mind rebels at what I see. It is not possible, it cannot be, that so many years of effort, of replanting the once ravaged two hundred acres, could be threatened with obliteration as a consequence of forty-five minutes of hail and wind!

"Dad, the window is broken in our room!"

The boys are awake, staring in disbelief at the new appearance outside, at the stripped pines, at the disarray and mess inside.

"We had a hailstorm. Look at the size of these hailstones. I saved them for you to see, in the freezer."

The ice balls covering the ground the night before were so many that there are still patches of stones among the trees the morning after.

*   *   *

It had cut a swath half a mile wide and many miles long. We had been in the path. A few miles away trailer houses had been tipped, the occupants injured. All of us in the line of the storm lost roofs, windows, possessions. The radio announcer terms it a tornado. I do not know if, technically, it really was. All I know, aside from the fright and the horror of it, and the helplessness, is that it will be many years before we can get a realistic assessment of damage.

The windows are repaired a few days later, and the roof has been reshingled. We have cleaned and fixed. And I am reminded of the limits of my ability to manage my world and my life. However I might try and struggle, a moth courting the candle of creation, my powers are finite, infinitesimal.

* * *

"I think these trees are going to make it," Tony sounds very sure. "It's been four or five years now since the storm."

"If the bugs don't get into them, or some sickness," David conditions the optimism.

"Have you considered becoming a lawyer when you grow up?" I ask David. "You could go into partnership with your mother. Offices downtown and all that."

But I am optimistic too, and reluctant to voice it for fear of putting a hex on the budding trees, as though I could control nature.

16 Bats in the Belfry and in the Bedroom

We all have an Achilles heel in our *sang-froid*. With Erica Jong it is flying; with my wife it is bats.

By definition such a fear has nothing to do with reason. It does not stem from the possibility, however slight, that bats can transmit rabies. This is a rare, slim chance. Any warm-blooded animal is susceptible and therefore a carrier in turn. Beavers can and do, a thought that brings me no pleasure. Humans can, and my father told of the soldier in World War I who sought to elude front line service in the Austrian army by claiming to have been bitten by a rabid dog; he in turn bit his friends and the several of them had to be sent off to the rear area hospital. Reason has nothing to do with it.

Nor is my wife's Batophobia related to unattractiveness on the part of bats. They are velvety soft, small, and pert. They catch many bugs. They are the original inventors of radar, far in advance of Germans or Americans or World War II.

And surely my wife knows as well as anyone that they do not descend on a pulsating neck in the dark of night and puncture veins to suck one's blood. She knows they do not turn into Count Dracula, though it seems to me that Batophobia becomes more acute after she has seen a horror movie on the late show.

*   *   *

"A bat! There's a bat in the house!"

The tocsin sounds: To arms, to arms! I muster to the fray, to return carrying my shield—or on it. No intermediate results, no compromises. So far as Peggy is concerned it is victory or death for me. (And the protection of the bedblanket over her head in the meantime.) No cheering, no encouragement. Just a barrage of questions. "Did you get him yet? Where is he? I can hear him, are you sure you got him?" "That was a mosquito, honey." "No, I'm sure I heard him. . . ." I do not respond to the inherent sexism that bats, the detested creatures, are masculine.

Is this rooted in childhood? Peggy's mother, a very hardy person who has endured difficulties, hardships, disasters with seeming equanimity, also goes to pieces at the sight of a bat. When Peggy was a child and a bat entered the premises, as they occasionally do, the whole family would be rousted to do battle. Brooms and other weapons in hand, every house light blazing, they would be commanded to the front and given explicit directions by her mother.

"There he is, hiding in the overhead light globe!"

"You missed him, he's behind the curtain rod!"

"Not that one, on the other wall, over the living room window!"

"He's in the kitchen now! Get him! Get him! Now he's in the broom closet!"

The orders come rapid fire until Peggy realizes that her mother is hidden under the bedding and can't see a thing.

"Mother, you can't even see the bat! Your head is covered!"

"I don't have to see it. I know it's there."

Peggy, brothers, sister, and father retire from the battlefield and hope for uninterrupted sleep the remainder of the night. Lights are doused and the bat re-emerges. Sensitive to light, it has hidden while the electric company profited. Now in the dark it whirrs around again, never bumping into anything due to the sensitive radar, making a soft, near-silent *whoosh* as it coasts about the premises seeking freedom.

"It's back. I told you you missed it!" Peggy's mother sounds general quarters again and the family comes tumbling out while her mother dives into the security of the batshelter under the sheets.

*   *   *

I do not understand how Peggy can laugh about her childhood experiences when she was a gladiator doing battle in her mother's behalf, while now it is she who suffers from Batophobia and directs our family in the conflict.

"You don't take me seriously!" she charges, shoving a news clipping under my nose. It is about a South American bat, supposedly quite large, that sucks blood. "Quite large" is an elastic term, and these apparently measure a few inches in wingspan compared to the tiny variety hereabouts; if indeed they do suck blood, the quantities must be tiny, measured in droplets. But in my wife's mind this species looms large, huge, maybe bald-eagle size. Count Dracula in cape, incisors protruding, heading for the Bemidji Blood Bank.

My reaction to bats is disappointing to my wife and to her mother, to put it mildly. It isn't that I am fond of them; I have no very positive feelings about them as, for instance, a neighbor who admires their unusual qualities and delicate bodies and catches the occasional stray in his house in gloved hands and sets it free. But neither are my feelings negative.

Once rousted, I turn on the lights in the bedroom, open the front door, and in a little while the bat flies to freedom and a repast of mosquitoes, allowing me to go back to sleep. At least this should allow me more sleep, but it is not to be.

"I can hear it again."

"Can't hear a thing."

"You need to get your ears checked. A hearing aid or something. I'm sure I can hear it!"

"You're imagining things."

"When you opened the door more came in than flew out."

"Ridiculous. They are sensitive to light and won't fly into it."

"There *is* a bat in the house! Maybe two or three!" The panic in her voice sends me off in search, but there are none.

"They've all gone to the belfry," I announce. "None here."

*   *   *

The small package is giftwrapped.

"For you," I tell Peggy.

"What's the occasion? Did I forget an anniversary or something?" she asks.

"No. Just a present. An unbirthday present."

Beneath the pretty paper is a box, about six inches by nine.

"What is this?" she peers inside, taking out some small wooden objects. Then she finds the instructions:

Northwoods Emergency Kit

IN THE EVENT OF BATS BREAK COVER.
REMOVE CROSS AND HEMLOCK STAKE.
GRASP CROSS IN LEFT, HEMLOCK STAKE IN RIGHT.
WAVE CROSS AND PLUNGE STAKE.

17 An Unorthodox Prayer

There goes the jet set, pursuing its geographic cure. Breakfast at Tiffany's, lunch in London, paparazzi in Rome, a tussle with photographers in Paris. It does not tempt me. The struggle part of life poses different pitfalls, other modes of escape for me.

As an adolescent I traveled widely, running away from my problems. It was supposed to be good for a young person to expand horizons and acquire knowledge by travel, though I knew and my parents knew that the real reason was avoidance of situations I could not, or did not want to resolve. Jets had not been invented then, and even if they had our family's circumstances would have precluded my traveling that way. I hitchhiked and worked my way across much of the country. I did learn a lot, not all of it good. I did not solve very much of what really bothered me, which I considered to be my parents, the school I attended, my being a small and puny kid with whom something, everything, was drastically wrong. The hitchhiker's version of the jet set did not work for me.

A slow learner who repeats his mistakes, I had to sample other methods of escape and avoidance that did not work either before it dawned on me (which many others seem to learn more quickly) that problems of jobs, wages, persons, and disasters were not what was truly bothering me. That overachieving, proving myself to others, proving myself to myself, being a hermit or being socially active, drinking a lot or taking tranquilizers solved nothing, but only compounded difficulties.

Perhaps it is a universal characteristic of humankind, something that lurks ever-present in the spirit of each of us. It is the proclivity for feeling worthless. Not as good as the mainstream of humanity. Cast off, detritus, debris, flotsam, jetsam on the surface of life.

Some people seem hard-shelled, the myriad assaults on one's self-esteem leaving them untarnished and unpitted, the hailstones having no apparent effect. Others protect themselves with defensive systems, seeking to manage and manipulate events, people, and relationships in an effort to stave off the inevitable, trying desperately not to feel pain and hurt. Yet others find anesthesia in alcohol, drugs, the chemicals that enable one to disengage from reality, to avoid living in the here and now. My way of joining the jetsam set is to withdraw into isolation, away from meaningful contact with others, and into myself, a snail on its odyssey of seeking self in further and further retreat into its shell, instead of out in the world among people and the rest of creation. Not that contemplation and time by oneself are bad; it is the withdrawal, the recoil from life, that is the danger for me.

*   *   *

"What's your name, little boy?" the first grade teacher asks on the opening day of school.

Silence. Huge dark eyes in a fawn face ringed by long black hair.

"What's your name?" Teacher more on edge, anxious to get on with all those good plans, those fine intentions, full of willingness to share, to impart, to teach.

Silence.

The child is sullen! Stupid? Deaf? Intransigent? Certainly sullen.

"Cat got your tongue? What's your name!" Teacher's frustration and anger are evident, as is disapproval of the child.

"He's Butch," another youngster volunteers.

There is a hint of a smile, at least of relief, around Butch's eyes. He has been saved the embarrassment of uttering his own name. He is an Indian child reared in a traditional home, learning that it is rude and improper to utter your own name.

But "Butch" isn't good enough. "Surely you have a given name? Come on now, what is your name?"

It is forced out of him. Jonathan.

It is an assault on the ego, on how we see ourselves and feel about ourselves. It is so for Jonathan-Butch, it is so for the teacher. It is born and bred of expectations and of cultural set, of ignorance, insensitivity, lack of understanding. In some ways these assaults happen to all of us — at the hands of parents, relatives, strangers, and events over which we have no control. And they leave their marks until we do to ourselves what life has done to us earlier.

Not far from us lives a woman who, to all appearances, has every gift for which one could wish to assure contentment in life. She is bright, she is attractive with a slim and full-figured body; her personality is pleasing, delighting to others. She has the advantage of being white, Anglo-Saxon, Protestant, which tend to keep the battering from society to a minimum. She has a good job with continuing career prospects, and she has the launching pad of an expanded family of solid, hardworking, blue-collar folks who have the respect of the community. Yet there is something in her make-up that says she lacks belief, trust, in herself, and that draws her to partners who beat her up. She detests being a battered wife and leaves her husband; yet her next one also batters her. Secretly she must detest herself to seek punishment like that.

No wonder the dictum at Delphi advised ancient Greeks seeking oracles to "Know Thyself." Every sin, vicissitude, every conflict and travail known to humans was known then and perhaps long before. We invent no evil and no proclivities; they have been generic in the species, part of us, for millennia. It seems that I struggle with something inherent and universal and timeless.

*   *   *

"You are a dreamer and don't want to admit it," writes a poet friend from Minneapolis. "You live in the northwoods and you write in this terse, condensed way that prunes out sentimentality and romanticism. Don't be afraid to admit that you dream!"

"I am a dreamer with a strong survival instinct," I write back. We both know, through reading each other's work and through correspondence, that my northwoods home and life-style are not a romantic idyll, a Waldenlike escape, although some seem to think that it is. It merely reflects a choice that I have made: This is how I want to live, and where. There is too much hard, grubby work; there are too many setbacks and difficulties in being a tree farmer to ever consider it a safe-haven, a refuge, a hermitage secure from life. It is simply a setting I have found comfortable, nourishing to my physical and spiritual needs. A place that enables my spirit and my body to come to terms with living, with the acceptance that there are no guarantees. Knowing that hailstorm, tornado, fire, illness, or bad luck can change anything overnight. But it is a place of beauty where I can seek to set a wholesome imprint on my surroundings by planting and harvesting trees, by safeguarding the environment at the same time that I enjoy its gifts and rewards. I am both steward of the land, and pilgrim on my rite of passage through life.

It is a place where personal relationships and extended family flourish for me. Where the daily routine of my life is such that when I wish to be part of the outdoors, I can do so in a natural and easy way, without extraordinary effort or artificiality. I can ski without driving long distances and buying admission and lift tickets. I can canoe, swim, fish much as I want to in season. Observer or participant, I can be outdoors at any time and conduct my very personal communion, can utter my private prayers on the riverbank, the lakeshore, or amid the cathedral of ancient trees on the hill.

My unorthodox prayers usually concern the wish to be aware and accepting, and appreciative, of life. I am here, at this moment, because of both a chain of countless generations reaching back into time and miasma beyond my reckoning or ken. Let me remember that I am a link in this chain, which continues into the future beyond my lifetime. I am part of the bucket brigade of creation, having had nothing to do with bringing it about or with the ending of it, being here through no act of my own, owing my presence to forces and powers I cannot comprehend, for my mind is incapable of dealing with the concepts of infinity, eternity, space. Yet I am here. I am.

AN UNORTHODOX PRAYER

I look up at the towering trees I did not plant, and down at the lower slopes where rises the plantation that I did, at the yearling bald eagle overhead, and I listen to the wind in the trees and the distant call of the loons. I hear the voices of children, their lives hopefully stretching into a future beyond mine, and I can open myself to the contact of life and creation, of friends, loved ones, of the yeasting that produced me, of which I am a part.

Not much of a prayer as these things go, but it helps me avoid the jetsam set.

18 Finding Symmetry in a Rock Pile

It has become increasingly important to me to strive for certain balances in my life, bringing symmetry to everyday living. Much of my work takes place indoors, all the more impelling me out of doors on walks, skis, snowshoes, by canoe. In order to suit me, these activities fit into the woof and warp of the day. Preferably, I would be able to step outside and do what I wish, as work and obligations allow.

It is the same with physical labor; working with wood, stone, and earth is counterweight to my intellectual pursuits, to the efforts in writing, in music, and in other fields. The contrast makes me appreciate the tactile and sensual rewards of physical work, even of drudgery. I relish the smell of cedar, pine, oak, and other woods in my carpentry pursuits, though the olfactory bouquet is no succor when I hit my finger with the hammer. Whether planting trees or spading the garden (which I do without significant enthusiasm, and amid much complaining), I am aware of the feel of the earth, of the variety of smells of the soil — dry, moist, lean, rich. It goes without saying that I am equally aware of the fertile manure pile that my wife had so thoughtfully delivered and dumped downwind from our bedroom window.

There is a particular fascination, bordering on a love affair, in working with stone. There have been occasions to help a neighbor clear rocks from a field, piling a cairn in a far corner; to build a stone wall; to split rock for fancy work; to construct a retaining wall to retard erosion in a cut. Now the time is here to rip-rap stone at each end of a culvert and along a steep bank bordering the driveway, at the place where it winds up the hill.

A neighboring farmer is happy to have his rockpile hauled out of the corner of a field and donate it to my needs.

"I know every one of those rocks personally," his wife tells me. "Picked most of them by hand, and a few we had to put chains around and pull with the tractor. Couple we had to use two tractors. Just be sure you don't let the cattle out when you open the gate. If they get in the green alfalfa this time of year they'll get sick and die."

I promise to be careful, to drive only along the fence line and not across the field, and to shut the gate entering and leaving.

*   *   *

I am lucky and get Andy Talevson to bring his big bulldozer with backhoe and his dump trucks, the condition being that I would work with him. The dump trucks look like museum pieces but the motors purr.

Andy is gray haired, pink cheeked, a stocky, short, bull of a man with the smile of a pixie; it starts with a twinkle and then unfolds slowly, but it is unstoppable once it begins, his personality warming everyone around. He is much more than a person involved in machinery and equipment, in grease and repairs and loud noises; like every human being, he has many facets to his self, a man of sensibilities and caring with an eye for beauty, a heavy equipment operator who is environmentalist, gardener, college student, parent. A man who would sooner lose time and squeak a huge machine between two trees than roar through and knock them over.

"First thing in the morning," says Andy, "you'll be ready."

It is a question, but said as a flat statement accompanied by arching eyebrows.

"I'll be ready." It is a safe commitment for me to make. When Andy says he'll start early in the morning it is about lunchtime for the rest of the world, but he will expect to work until it is pitch dark or later. It is just that his concept of the workday is a bit off the norm. But he is the best, and I cherish him besides.

*   *   *

FINDING SYMMETRY IN A ROCK PILE

In midafternoon the loaded trucks arrive. I had begun to fret by then, expecting a phone call to the neighboring farm to help Andy, his son, and his helpers. But they apparently concluded I would be more hindrance than help, and they surprise me with the first installment of boulders. Andy untwines himself from the cab of the bigger truck and inspects the terrain, Napoleon at Austerlitz preparing for the battle.

"There's some peat down there," he announces. "We could put a few really big ones there, spot them around, for a rock garden. Flowers." This has nothing to do with rip-rapping the culvert, where receding spring ice and runoff pose a problem, or with the erosion along the driveway. Andy just takes it for granted he will take care of these, and he has his eye on the aesthetics of the job.

"Bring me some big ones," he instructs his helpers. "From the north end of the rockpile." He climbs on the bulldozer, parked there the day before, and starts the machine. Piles, mounds of stone are pushed to the culvert ends and rolled down. How will I ever get some of the bigger ones, weighing several hundred pounds, in position? I am reluctant to ask Andy to help with individual stones; he is already doing more than I had expected.

"When the backhoe is attached I'll spot the bigger ones," he calls down from the roaring machine. "Don't bother with them now. Just figure out where you want them. There's a pretty one, I'll just roll it aside for the rock garden." He is off, pursuing his vision of a Japanese contemplation stone weighing nearly half a ton that he seems to think will be beautiful amid the ferns. It is a whitish granite, almost limestone in color, a prehistoric egg among craggy and odd-shaped greens, pinks, and ochres.

I pause from my end of the job, placing stones in a slanting wall from the creek up toward the driveway, anchoring stone upon stone, shoveling sand to lay each one, stepping the next stone up. They feel rough, but a pattern, a system evolves in how they should go together. Andy has infected me with the vision, the sense of how it might, how it should be.

"Could we take four big ones out to the end of the drive-way," I ask, "where the kids wait for the schoolbus? They'd each have a sitting rock."

"We'll pick some smooth ones," he answers, casting his eye around. The trucks keep hauling, and he tells the drivers he wants more "big ones."

"And next time dump them farther up the drive," he in-structs. "I'll spot for you when you come back." He has very definite ideas.

Several loads later he has found the perfect sitting stones, and he picks them out with delicate movements, handling the con-trols of the rumbling and roaring monster he drives with the delicacy of a watchmaker.

*   *   *

One boulder too large for me to move catches my eye. It is blue? Green? When the rain has washed it the true color will be discernible. There are deep, parallel ridges grooved in it, about an inch deep, nearly two inches wide. It is a piece of granite bedrock that had been beneath a glacier, and through the inex-orable, slow movement of the glacial mass tens of thousands of years ago, smaller stones caught in the glacier bottom had gouged, grooved the pattern.

I manage to tip the mass over, and find similar grooves on the sides of the rock as well.

"Hey Andy," I call. "Here's one with deep glacial rill."

He stops the machine, dismounts to look, and we contem-plate this ancient piece of original life and earth, this mother of us all, welded of tiny pieces and bits of rock and matter by vol-canic lava, by the action of some Mount St. Helens billions of years ago in some Precambrian eruption; then cooled, buried, upheaved, grilled, ultimately broken, working its way up in a farmer's field over the hundreds of millions of years. It is a re-minder of the incredible forces and the time that has elapsed in the lifeflow and processes that produced us.

We go back to our work, then the machine is throttled down again.

"Where do you want that one?" Andy asks. I had not said anything but he knew I would want it for my own, in some private place among huge pines, a centerpiece in the cathedral of trees to look at, to contemplate, at times sit upon.

I look up at the hill, and he nods. "I think I can get it there without disturbing anything."

19 A Fowl Idea

It is supposed to be a virtue to be charitable. Kind, thoughtful, generous, patient, and loving. But there are limits. Like poultry, regular or webfooted, no matter what Ducks Unlimited has to say.

I draw the line at chickens, stupid and smelly creatures that peck your feeding hand just because you are trying to snatch an egg from beneath their south end as they face north. As a youngster I had to care for chickens when my mother thought that Dad needed a new hobby, and he opted for these critters. He armed himself with literature from the county agent, which he turned over to me with a regretful look on his face.

"I'd do it, but I've got to work overtime at the shop," he said, meaning that he wanted me to construct the wire mesh floor frames. The idea was that droppings would fall through the mesh, which was mounted on two-by-two frames, to the floor beneath to be recaptured for the garden, while the chickens would remain pristine. There were two troubles with the scheme. Dad always had to work overtime when one of these projects came up, and you could not argue with the economics of it: Money was scarce, overtime even scarcer. It was just that the overtime only seemed to happen when mother had generated a new hobby for him. The second problem was that the floor screens, once completed, did not work for our chickens the way they did in the literature.

Our chickens were heavy-footed. They tramped, stomped, and trod until the wire mesh sagged, the droppings were compacted, and the hard-packed stuff smelled to the high heavens. Our chickens were just as filthy as everybody else's.

"Dad, I think your garden is ready for the chicken fertilizer," I announce, "and I've got schoolwork to do."

"Oh, well, the garden could use it, but I've got to work overtime tonight." So much for my attempt to finesse the removal of the manure. Money wins over mind every time.

Dad loved those chickens, overfeeding them, clucking at them, collecting eggs (when the hens were not in a mood to sit on them). But he had to work overtime when it came to cleaning out the poultry house or killing and plucking them. I did enjoy the latter chore, hoping for the day when the last one would be gone and mother would devise a new and different hobby for him.

Ultimately we got out of the chicken business and he took up bees, and he had to work overtime when they swarmed or it was time to extract honey. They were very mean then. Fate avenged me when Dad pulled on an old pair of pants with a buttoned fly, uniformed himself with bee net and gloves to go out and inspect them, and they promptly penetrated his clothing. He moved very fast, and we got out of the bee business shortly after.

*   *   *

"We could save a lot of money by raising our own chickens," says my wife.

"No way!"

"No way, no way, no way," chant the twins, now two years old, while Tony and David smirk at each other. They have heard this tape replayed often, including the debating points about fresh eggs, meat unpolluted by chemicals, living off the land, and so forth.

"All right, we'll get ducks and geese," says Peggy.

"They are cute," Tony reinforces her.

"Watch it, kid, or you'll be taking care of them," I warn him.

"They are not cute," Tony gives in.

"So cuddly and yellow!" David apparently does not know when he is well off, despite my warning scowl.

"Cuddy, cuddy, cuddy," chant Micah and Megan.

I shoot a poisonous look at them, which has no effect.

"Ducks," says Peggy. "And geese."

I say something unprintable, which the twins repeat over and over.

*   *   *

The soft yellow balls of fluff arrive inconveniently, unexpectedly, in the midst of a family crisis, one of those periodic moments when all goes awry with schedule conflicts, unanticipated work demands, and an intemperate fit of pique on the part of the water pump, which seems to have a perverse sense of timing all its own. None of this stops the children from ohhing and ahhing or Peggy from clucking at them. Infuriating. *I* want the mothering, never mind ten ducks and two geese.

Words drift toward my ears, penetrate my consciousness: "Adorable . . . cute . . . peep-peep . . . will you carry in the fifty-pound bag of feed from the car?"

Peggy begins a ledger sheet. She is out to prove to me that the raising of web-footed poultry is cost effective. The sheet is posted above their shelter in the entryway of our house.

"Where is the brooder lamp?" I ask. "You didn't put that down. Or the fencing for their pen, or the water dispenser." The roll of fencing is outside, awaiting their growth to the time, devoutly anticipated by me already, when they move out to the yard.

"I'm only putting down the costs of raising them," replies my wife, the set of her chin announcing a defensive posture. I know that she knows that you have to apportion capital costs, but her poultry bookkeeping is confined strictly to the direct operating costs, and excludes indirect costs and capital outlays. This is the pitfall, the nemesis of the "live off the land cult." Many such cultists have come to our area over the years, most have failed and left; those who succeed and stay do so not as the result of animal husbandry or farming, but income derived from other work. Peggy knows this but her poultry ledger does not reflect it.

Within two days the cute peepers in our entryway emit an odor that turns to stench, exacerbated by the heat lamp hung over their pen.

"They have to be cleaned," I demand. But Tony flees, David has to pack belongings for going to camp, the twins would hug them to death. . . .

"Let Micah and Megan do it!" I suggest, and Peggy assumes a protective stance in front of the pen as though to shield the web foots from Armageddon.

"You can surely do it," I arch eyebrows at Peggy.

"I would, but I have a case in court, and a brief to finish, and a client is coming in." All at once, no doubt. And she is dressed for town and it sounds suspiciously like my father's long ago "overtime." Life repeats, in this instance ad nauseam. The cuddlies really do stink. In self defense I clean their pen, which faces our entry door from the inside, and hugs the doorway into the kitchen. They peep, crowd, and cluster, peck at each other, and don't appeal to me at all.

I hope the cat will take a lively interest, but he circumvents them, wrinkling his nose.

"Duck soup," I say to the cat. "Peking. Orange. Stuffed. Roast." He walks off in a dudgeon. "Glazed?" But he has gone.

*   *   *

They grow. They eat twice as much as Peggy had anticipated, and meanwhile the price of feed goes up. Even after three weeks the yellow fluff has long been gone and they are gangly adolescents, unappealing in every sense.

"They should go outside," I suggest once again.

"It still gets cold at night," Peggy protests.

Tony worries: "There are foxes, skunks. . . ."

I mentally add, with some wishfulness, weasels, muskrats, snapping turtles and, in vain, the cat.

The smell finally gets to everyone. Even Micah and Megan, passing the overheated pen are announcing, "Ishy. Pew. Pew." The time comes for the big move, with fence posts and fencing piled outside in the yard, near the creek.

"I'd love to help but I have to work overtime tonight," says Peggy before I can say the same.

*   *   *

It is easier now that they are in the outdoors pen. Less offensive. Also, they are too big to sit in the water dispenser or in the food tray. However, all predators stay away from them. My hopes are raised by a circling hawk; he dives, he comes closer, he flies away. Our web-footed friends are saved by . . . a smell? If my family thinks this is bad, I say to myself, just wait until it is time for plucking, when I plan to be far away, out of town, abroad.

A friend of mind was bedeviled as a youngster by a mean goose on the family farm. The goose would chase him, peck him whenever he appeared outdoors, making life miserable for him until Thanksgiving. Then my friend went into the yard insouciantly, passing close to the pen. When the goose came charging, sticking his head through the fence to get a good bite of those passing legs, my friend grasped the vulnerable head and neck and dispatched the beast. How long, oh how long, to Thanksgiving.

Tony posts a sign in the yard: Beware of Goose. Friends coming to play bridge comment on the sign with amusement, safe from our growing poultry by virtue of the fence, but make some remarks about the new odors in our yard.

As we play cards, someone remarks that we could use better lighting.

"Got just the thing," I say, returning with the brooder lamp, which I hang over the card table. "There, that should do it."

We are warmed, illuminated by the fixture no longer needed by our web-footed friends. Since Peggy won't amortize the contraption in her "living off the land" scheme, I may as well put it to more versatile use. Country life, living off the land, is not as simple as it is cracked up to be. But it does train you to be flexible while waiting for Thanksgiving.

20 Drought of the Spirit Hits the Mailbox

The hot searing drought is a dispiriting, depressing time. Day lapses into day without rainfall and the moisture seeps, evaporates invisibly from the soil. It is obvious at first among the surface-feeding plants, as the lawn grass and vegetable garden become parched and brown; then the trees show their thirst, leaves losing luster, then hinting that they may curl and turn brown. Even the bold spring candles of the pines' new growth show a droop, a listlessness. Flowage in the creek has stopped, a bit of seepage during the night, but nothing in the day. It is a time that will be noted by future foresters examining tree rings as a bad year; the growth ring for this drought year will be a microscopic band, compared to the wide ring indicating last year's lush and dramatic growth.

Whatever the survival, there will be, already is, damage and setback. In the past there have been years when drought brought not only extreme fire hazards and discomforts, but killed thousands of seedlings we had planted; once we had to do over after putting in 65,000 pines.

As days pass one another and the wishful thinking of weather forecasters comes to naught, as one wet weather system after another just misses our part of the country and the morning weather maps on television fail to show relief, the dust and sand on the road, in the fields, becomes finer, more pernicious, wafts farther in the wind.

We sit in the yard relishing the small comfort of evening cool in the unremitting dryness, the children less troubled by it all than we who have lived with drought and its consequences before and have a baseline of experience and expectation. A vehicle is being driven down the country road, apparently at high speed. We can see the dust plume rising high, a miniature tornado above the road, even though the road itself is out of our view, screened by trees.

The sound of a crash followed by loud voices, curses wafting across to our ears clearly. It sounds mean, vicious. I hasten up the drive, concerned someone might have been hurt. As I emerge at the end of the driveway where it meets the dusty country road, a pickup truck disappears from view, leaving behind a residue of dust that seems to hang in midair a long time, a tiny Alamagordo.

The mailbox has been knocked down, the post splintered. From the tracks it appears someone has driven off the road and directly at the mailbox, swerved into and then out of the ditch to do so. Purposely? It would be difficult along the long stretch of unobstructed road to drive off the road at just this one place. Footprints show that two persons had gotten out of the truck, walked about the place, then gotten back in to drive away. There is no sign of the mailbox itself. The heavy post on which it had been mounted, set deeply into the ground, is totally splintered.

I hurry back to the house, get in my car, and set off in pursuit, my feelings fueled by anger at what seems a wanton act of destruction, a denigration of my own labor and effort, without even the courtesy or effort to inform me, much less make amends. The truck tracks are distinctive, the tire patterns discernible even in the fine dust. They turn off a mile away onto a service track leading to the canoe landing. This is a lovely place, a high bluff overlooking a bend of the Mississippi, which is maintained by the Department of Natural Resources for the benefit of canoe parties traveling up and down the river. It is a marvelous campsite and rest stop set amid pines and large clusters of birch and a listening post into the sounds of the ecosystem, a viewing place that includes a deer ford, a flyway for ducks, osprey, eagles, herons. At night one can hear the screeching of wildcats, the bark of foxes, the slap of beaver tails. Long ago it was lookout, stopover place for Indians on their way to and from ricing, sugaring, hunting, on seasonal migrations. Then it was logged, became tax forfeited, and into the hands of the state, which elected to make of it a canoe landing so as to perpetuate the beauty and usefulness of it.

Occasionally roisterers and drinking parties penetrate the place and bedevil the campers, even canoe parties of children from nearby summer camps. Motorcyclists try the tender trails and erosion is setting in. And the birch trees are girdled by people peeling bark all around them, leading to the eventual death of the trees. Beer cans, litter, and spent shell casings from target shooting are scattered about. I have come to wish that the road into the place would be blocked off except for maintenance vehicles so that the place would not be utterly devastated by hooligans. Now I follow the track to find the people who have wrecked by mailbox, my mind subliminally noting that in the dense forest along the track the drought has wrecked less damage than elsewhere, the root systems and ground cover acting as a blanket retarding evaporation of ground moisture.

I hear them before I see them. They are taunting, shouting obscenities at a handful of frightened youngsters clustered about three tents, a party of canoe-campers whose counselor is hard put to shield, reassure the children while trying to get rid of the tormentors.

The truck is occupied by two young men in their late teens. Between them sits an excited ten- or eleven-year-old whom they encourage to join in heckling the campers. I walk over, see the empty, open, and full beer cans in the cab of the truck. And the mailbox, apparently taken along as a trophy. I am furious now, enraged by their frightening the children, by the awful example they are setting to the youngster in the truck whom they prod toward antisocial behavior.

Ordinarily I am discreet enough to stay away from drunks who are acting out and leave such matters to the law. After all, I have their license number now and the sheriff could handle it. Not this time.

"That's my mailbox you knocked over," I tell them.

They are very drunk, sixteen- or seventeen-year-olds, thick-tongued and glassy-eyed but still drinking.

"Yeah, we're sorry about that," one says. "A deer jumped out and we tried to miss it and hit your mailbox."

I had seen no deer tracks nearby, and take this for a patent lie.

"Then why did you take the mailbox?"

"We meant to come back and fix it."

"Now's as good a time as any. You fix it or the sheriff will see to it that you do."

They leave to obtain a new post at the home of nearby relatives.

The camp counselor comes over. "I don't know if I should bring the children here any more, it isn't the first time we've had trouble."

Such a perfect place to participate in the outdoors.

"You'll run into drunks and meanness wherever you go," I answer. "It can happen in the city, and it does, and it can happen here. I can't tell you what to do about your camp policies, but I feel that you can't surrender the world to the hooligans."

Back at my mailbox two very drunk teenagers stagger about, trying to cope with the setting of a new post. I furnish a post-hole digger and watch as they dig into the dry, sifting sand. Both boys reek of alcohol, then one steps aside to be sick. I wish a bit more drought into their lives, a little less for the rest of us.

"Is this deep enough?"

I try the post in the hole they have dug.

"No, the mailman can't reach it. The box has to be level with the height of the car window."

They dig more, feeling very sick, wobbly, taking time out to retch in the ditch. What malaise of the mind, what drought of the spirit, is it that leads such nice looking, promising youngsters to become destructive of themselves and of others? I gather from their conversation that this kind of drinking is a commonplace occurrence with them.

They finally finish the job. It should have taken fifteen minutes but in their condition requires much longer.

"Are you going to file charges?" one of them asks before leaving.

"No reason to. You made restitution. If there's a next time I'll know where to find you."

"There won't be a next time."

"Maybe not around my place, but if you drink like that there'll be more next times."

They leave in a swirl of dust. I notice stray clouds as I walk home. We've had these teasers all spring, into the summer, but no significant rain. Some day, maybe weeks, maybe months, the weather cycle will change, but there is no telling how much damage will have been incurred by then.

Some day, perhaps, the emotional, the spiritual climate will change for the two young men and they will come to accept life and living not as a perpetual drought that has to be moistened with ethyl alcohol in its various forms, an anesthesia. I can pace my own life to deal with the periodic droughts in the weather cycle and its consequences, but it is impossible to put a rain gauge on a human spirit. We humans can be so destructive and do so much harm to ourselves and to others; just these two people in one random evening have impacted the lives of the youngster with them, whom they have instructed, enticed so badly. They have frightened a group of children who had been bent on an experience intended to enrich their love of the out-doors.

The drought upon the land will end in time. There is no assurance that the drought of the spirit will; I only know that it can.

21 The Berry-Raiding Parties

It is an atavistic urge within us, a primordial instinct, that impels us as the wild berries ripen. We stock the family car with berry pails, mosquito repellant, and blueberry trays. Sometimes we set out having first scouted a plentiful supply all in one place; more often we seize the opportunity of the moment, the occupants of the car spilling out and fanning through the woods at a promising spot while en route on errands, visiting, or poking along back roads and trails.

The word *Berry* is capitalized in our family, in writing and in speech, and used generically, it being understood what the variety of the moment is. The phenomenon begins with wild strawberries, graduates to raspberries, blackberries, then blueberries, chokecherries, pin cherries, wild plums, high bush cranberries, and on rare occasions wild grapes. We speak of Berries as vital to palate and pocketbook, but I have noticed that we go picking and putting up even when some of last year's leftover stock is still on the shelves. It is not always cost effective, and at times we have jams, jellies, and sauces from previous years. The truth must emanate from something deeper, more fundamental, than supply and demand.

David has the knack for strawberries, sparse this year, and can find them when no one else sees a single one.

"Not a good year," he reports. "Can't find any."

But his mouth is ringed in red and for once he does not make a beeline for the refrigerator when entering the house. He is holding out on us. And this is the boy who only two years ago courted instant execution at the hands of the rest of the family when he blurted out, in a roomful of company, that we had

95

been Berry picking that day and gave away the precise location. Peggy looked daggers at him, my hands arched into talons, Tony went for the baseball bat, and David cringed. It is a cardinal rule even among relatives, much less friends, not to give away such secrets.

Tony and I are the blueberry freaks, both for picking and for eating, although Peggy is the best finder. She has a finely tuned radar that enables her to say, "Pull over. No, not here, back up a few feet."

Inevitably the place will yield Berries, usually far back from the road and out of sight. It is uncanny, an extrasensory gift, though she is not all that fond of blueberries and prefers cranberries above all else.

* * *

It is fall, and the telephone rings. Peggy is en route to a business appointment and late, she explains. She is calling from a country store miles from anywhere, between two towns.

"Can you meet me here?" she asks. "I'm in high heels and nylons and there is this tremendous patch of cranberries. I can get the ones on the high ground but I can't get into the swamp."

I find her car, then see her a ways off in the brush bending high bush cranberry branches, greedily picking the deep orange and red Berries. Her hat is full and in the car, and she is now picking into her briefcase, the contents of which are perched precariously on the dash. Peggy is about cranberries the way the Hunt Brothers are about silver.

"I got all I can," she pants, "but there are more out in the swamp and I'm late."

I watch her pick her way out of the brush, still immaculate, the briefcase in hand. It's not crazy; it's just Berry Time.

Berries were a staple of Indian cuisine in the olden days. Dried, they could be stored for long periods and then served in stews; or pounded into pemmican with meat and fat; or served with a topping of maple syrup. Ojibwe diet was quite varied and imaginative. The penchant for wild fruit, particularly Berries, is found in virtually all cultures and ethnic stocks, and somehow our multicultural family has been endowed, perhaps genetically, with the Berrying urge from all possible sources.

We make jams and jellies, we freeze, we can. We gorge. Tony races in the house with the first half cup of blueberries (does that boy ever walk?) and makes blueberry pancakes for the two of us. The next two cups go for blueberry pie. With Peggy, cranberries arouse the appetite for leg of lamb garnished with Cumberland sauce, cranberry jelly instead of currant. The twins are entirely indiscriminate and take on all comers in the way of wild Berries, rejecting only storebought fruit (other than grapes) during Berry Season; Micah is showing signs of inclining toward raspberries. With David it is hard to tell what comes first; he is in and out of the refrigerator and freezer like a yo-yo and it is impossible to establish what all he ingests in the course of a day, or where his priorities lie. I think he favors raspberries and strawberries, but I can't keep up with him.

Once in a while you hit a wonderful Berry patch, so good that you dream, fantasize, talk about it long afterwards. There was a blueberry patch far off in the bog country one year, the ground a deep carpet of moist, cool moss while overhead a bright sun in clear blue skies heated, baked us squatting in the comfortable marsh. It was a world of contrasts and penetrating smells, for even the ripe blueberries give off their odor along with the dank moss, the occasional clusters of bright red lingenberries, the swamp tea, and distant smell of pines. We lose sight of each other, hear occasional plunking of Berries falling into pails, soft movements as pickers shift position. The Berries are so plentiful that you move from place to place only to stretch legs; you could sit in one place for a long time, keeping on picking merely by squidgying around. It is a sea of blue atop the deep green of the thick moss. I have returned to this place several times, but once the Berries had frozen out in spring, probably about the time they were blooming. Another time the bog was flooded during a very rainy early summer. It was never good picking there again, but I still dream of that one marvelous time.

As with hunting, garnering firewood, and other local folk

practices, there is a certain mystique to Berrying that involves the art of lying with a straight face.

"Bet you had to go pretty far for those cranberries," a cousin probes. He has never told me where he finds those large quantities of huge blueberries and I'm not about to give away my sources. But we keep playing the game that seldom brings rewards but is always fun.

"All the way in Third River country," I lie.

"D'you go by Pennington?"

"Yup." I follow this with some more misdirections, specific enough to sound plausible, otherwise leading to nonexistent spots. In actuality we had found the cranberries while stopping at a country store for a Sunday newspaper.

"Cranberries!" yells David, pointing across the road where brush and bushes hang over the ditch.

All of us rush there, Berry pails flying, leaving the car parked in front of the store while the storekeeper gazes after us in puzzlement.

Tony, David, and I are out for late-season blueberries in a jackpine woods only a few miles from home. The crop is spotty but the farther we go into the woods the better the picking becomes. By lunch time we have several gallons.

"Time to quit," I call out. "If we go any farther we'll be in Wally Smith's backyard."

We can't see the house but I know the area and we are getting mighty close. Then, as usually happens when you decide to quit, you find a few more patches of extra good Berries.

Back at the car we dump the Berries into my automated cleaning machine: trays made of quarter-inch wire mesh, two-inch sides bent up. Leaves, sticks, green Berries fall through the mesh and the ripe Berries stay behind in the tray without being crushed. Cleaning the Berries then becomes a simple task: A tray is tilted on the picnic table, one end propped by an upended cookpot. The ripe, clean Berries then tumble off the lower end of the tray into a waiting pan, so clean they do not have to be washed or picked over.

Driving home we meet Wally Smith coming toward us. We

pull off the road, as does he. His car is jammed with family and they, too, are returning from Berry picking.

"Where've you been?" I ask.

"Way up toward Red Lake," he lies. Several full pails of Berries are in view, about as good and as much as we harvested this morning. "How'd you make out?"

"Fair, fair," I lie. "Been near Badoura."

Tony and David wince, kick each other. Badoura is forty miles from where we picked.

We exchange pleasantries, continue on our diverging ways. I chuckle all the way home thinking of Wally Smith driving miles and miles for Berries when a bumper crop was a few feet from his back fence.

At home we set up shop on the picnic table. The perfect blueberries rattle into kitchen containers, cascading off the tilted trays. This batch is destined for sauce.

"Look pretty good," Peggy comments. "You all did well for the short time you were out." She is such a good picker that her praise means a lot.

"By the way," she adds. "I thought I saw Wally Smith's car parked up the road most of the morning. Where the trail goes to the west forty. He must have had his kids along judging from the noise. What do you suppose they were doing?"

Red Lake indeed! He'd been in my backyard! While I was in his!

"Picking mushrooms, I suppose," I mutter, leaning over the trays.

"Where did you go today?" Peggy inquires.

"Oh, down near Badoura."

22 Silent Despair

For two weeks she lives in a college dormitory free of the chores of the farm, of motherhood, of wifery, and breathes the heady atmosphere of the intensive writer's conference. She works with playwrights, authors, fellow conferees, and rediscovers her ability to write short stories and poetry. She can hold her own, do a bit better than the school teachers, writers, housewives, and others who make up the student body.

Her husband drives the eighty miles one way from the desolate little farm to attend conference dinners, readings, performances. He brings their little boy. When she reads one of her stories before an audience of writers, conferees, and townspeople, many of her friends and relatives attend, but they step into the hallway for cigarettes as the readings are given, mutter to each other, and the husband seems more concerned about his wife's new acquaintances than with the story she reads.

"You're not wearing a bra!" he hisses at her in the hallway after the reading, even as congratulators crowd around.

"What an enchanting, thought-provoking story," says the middle-aged nun who has been teaching the course on writing for children.

"A beautiful piece of work," adds the head of the university English department, shaking the author's tiny hand. She is petite, gamin, with blond bangs and hazel eyes. She must have been pretty as a young girl. Over thirty now, she is pert, attractive. At the moment her eyes glitter and she is on top of the world, a promise, a potential of creative ability tested, confirmed by critics with high standards.

"Who was that man?" The husband's voice is no longer a whisper and people turn to look. "He was looking at you. . . ."

"He directed the conference. He is dean of the English department."

The husband moves as if to speak, reconsiders, his grip tightens on her arm and his knuckles whiten as he glares, mute, brimming with anger.

"You're hurting my arm!" Her face is torn, the mouth smiling at the congratulators who continue to crowd, the eyes welling with tears.

"This is all dumb, it doesn't mean anything," the husband says. "Ah hell, it'll all be over day after tomorrow and you'll be back home."

The instructor of the fiction writing seminar approaches. He is a short, affable man, professorial in appearance, owl eyes peering through thick-lensed glasses.

"Good work," he smiles. "You have a major talent, need an agent. Not now perhaps, but in a year or two if you keep writing. I'll give you the name and address of my agent in New York, and I'll tell her about you. I think she will be interested in you."

The husband wheels and walks away, the tight yellow T-shirt emphasizing sunburned, muscular shoulders and arms, his tight-fitting clothes suggesting a narcissistic macho swagger.

There is a party after the readings. She is surrounded by well-wishers, he is alone; she has not yet introduced him to any of her new friends and acquaintances, although he has come to visit several times. They are a wine and cheese crowd, he is Old Boy and beer. He knows no one, feels ill at ease, inferior.

The crowd is four deep around the serving table, she in the midst of the group.

"Hand me a beer, will ya?" he calls to her, but she does not acknowledge the request. He asks a second, a third time before she reaches for a can, which she hands to him across two other people without looking at him.

They part later that evening in front of her dormitory. They have both drunk too much, been cruel to each other, and now he drives off without goodnight or goodbye, leaving her standing at the curb.

*   *   *

It is not just the overload of farmwork and household chores that have kept her from the writing for so long, this college drop-out waif from a broken motherless home, this St. Louis expatriate living on a far northern farm carved out amid the pines and granite near the Canadian border.

It is not just the isolation from intellectual stimulus, from a cultural environment conducive to creativity, that have kept her from it.

"He puts me in a box!" she wails after the party in her dormitory room. "With his jealousy and his suspicions. Any time I try to do something I get punished. If I read a book, I'm not paying attention to him. If I try to write, he says I neglect the child. But I don't neglect my child! I'm the one who plays with him, reads to him, tends him every day; he never does. And when he says those things, then . . . afterwards . . . he puts his arm around me and he says he loves me. How can he say he loves me when he is destroying me?"

Other student-writers comfort her, some of them older women who have gone through their own growing up, maturing, adjusting. The sobbing, the hysteria subside in time.

"Your story was really about you and your little boy," a woman friend remarks. "The man had a minor role in it, that of the villain. I wonder how your husband feels about that?"

The games that masochists and sadists play are at times subtle, at times overt, but always cruel. Yet there is an old adage that for every castrator there is a castratee. It can become a *pas de deux* of despair, the dancers pirouetting, spiraling ever downward. Clutching at each other at the very moment they hate each other most.

*   *   *

Who locked the door of her gilded cage, if that squalid, struggling dairy farm can be called that? Who put her in a cage in the first place? Did he? Did she? Both? Knowingly or unwittingly? One can speculate her seeking affirmation of her womanliness, of her womanhood, from a macho male; speculate that behind his well-advertised physique lurks an insecure person who needs to master and control his wife or else, he fears, he would not be able to secure her love. And so she lives the life of a psychologically battered wife, the very opposite of what she had craved; and he lives in a world of her contempt, resentment, and growing hatred, instead of the affection and admiration he desires.

A marriage relationship that does not work, commonplace as it may be, is always the source of pain and unhappiness. When the by-product is also the stifling and possible destruction of a potentially major talent, such a situation approaches the tragic.

The great harm is not only to the individuals involved, not only to the child who is beaten, the spouse who is battered. The great harm is not only to society when such situations spawn children who in turn grow up to become batterers or battered, veritable progenitors of Jukes and Kalikaks. The great harm is also in the loss, the stultification of talent, such as that of the potential short-story writer and poet. For the essential function of art, beyond entertainment, is to make us a mite better, richer in spirit and in mind, than we were before we saw that painting, regarded that sculpture, read that book, beheld that show, witnessed that play.

*   *   *

There is little predictability about the scenario of human lives. No one can say, looking at the future, that the little story writer will mature, will ripen, will be strong enough to be wife, mother, and creative artist; that she will draw from inner strength the knowledge that she is a whole person and does not need to draw that information exclusively from her macho husband; that she will abandon that false notion that she is inherently inadequate, bad, and needs to be punished either by the partners she seeks or the behavior she incites in them. No one can say that he will grow up, will find out that he is of worth and comparable to his human peers, and deserving of love and affection in his own right without having to coerce, to browbeat such manifestations from others. It could go badly for one or for both; the statistics of our courts, our battered womens' centers, our alcoholism and drug programs, indicate that many people do not win in this struggle with themselves. There are many lives lived in silent despair, and stillborn talents are legion.

It is in the overcoming of our human bondage, of our traps and imprisonments, that there arises the true challenge of life, the true test of mettle, the difference between existing and living.

Happily ever after?

23 A Boy Learns To Steward Land and Time

"When can I go on a canoe trip with you?"

"When you can swim."

"I can swim now."

"Dog paddle. I mean swim well."

A familiar exchange as the boy grows, develops through the years. But the time comes and he becomes a proficient swimmer, a sparkling nine-year-old, soon to be ten, who wants to ply his dreams of glory.

*   *   *

There is a residue of chill in the early morning air, a promise of warmth, although the partial overcast suggests that it may become windy, blustery.

"Do you think it will get gusty?" I ask the park ranger, a lanky, bearded man collecting canoes, paddles, life jackets, and visitors at the Lake Kabetogama shore of Voyageurs National Park. But of course he has no secret foreknowledge of the weather, and can only guess and gauge on the basis of experience.

"We can stay close in among the islands if it blows up later in the day," he says. He is Lee Grim, biology instructor at the International Falls Community College, an experienced naturalist and researcher, doctoral candidate, who spends summers working for the park service.

Our flotilla of four canoes pushes off. Lee and a young man with a day off from his resort job lead the way, followed by a young couple on their first visit to Voyageurs. Behind them, paddling a sawtooth pattern, is a couple from north-central Kansas escaping the heat wave there; they are in their late fifties, sampling life with enthusiasm. David and I make the fourth pair.

We find our stroke and I keep quiet in the stern while David plunges his paddle vigorously in the bow, undoubtedly among the voyageurs of the fur trade by now, mentally setting out for Athabaska; he has to get there before the winter freeze-up and deliver trade goods to far-flung posts, returning with furs in the spring after wintering in the interior.

Actually we are only crossing the few miles of Kabetogama, heading for the peninsula and a hike into the wilderness interior. But boys' dreams must be made possible.

"Slow down the stroke," I finally plead, feeling my breath come faster, "we have to pace ourselves to paddle all day."

We coast to an island where osprey nest and the adult birds come wheeling overhead, warning us off with shrill calls. We can see their young perching on the nest edge atop a large dead tree, peering curiously.

"They are within a week or two of fledging," Lee explains. "Learning to fly," he adds as the Kansans look at him inquiringly.

One's respect for Lee increases on acquaintance. He is an expert in several fields, including ornithology, geology, ecology, the ecosystems and natural history of the Rainy Lake area, where he grew up. And he is invariably patient, considerate, instructing the Kansans in paddling technique and answering their questions, helping the young couple identify birds, encouraging David.

The osprey follow us, soaring and screaming, almost eagle-size overhead, and finally leave off as we pass their territory and continue across Kabetogama. Islands that had blended into mainland become distinct as we near, paddle by, and then blend into mainland again in retrospective.

Lee scans the sky for signs of eagle; there are three established nests nearby that, inexplicably, seem to have produced no young this year and he hopes to find a new nest or two, built by the broods of prior years.

*   *   *

Voyageurs Park has the dramatic beauty of Boundary Waters and the Quetico-Superior, yet it is different in a subtle way. Perhaps this is because the new park is encompassed by four large lakes, while BWCAW to the east contains many smaller lakes. And then there is the landmass of the Kabetogama Peninsula, erstwhile home of elk and caribou (which are extinct in the region), and now terrain for moose and white-tailed deer. The peninsula can be reached only across water in summer; across ice in winter.

We land at the end of a bay, beach the canoes, and hike into the interior to Locator Lake. The trail winds uphill and down, around beaver ponds, diagonally across escarpments, among birch popple, spruce; from an overlook we see a stand of black spruce in the lowland, dramatic dark green among the lighter shades of the other trees. Our trail has been used by deer, moose, and smaller game. Partridge fly up, scuttle among the brush, and nearby a pileated woodpecker chucks at us. Lee mimics the bird calls and I cannot distinguish between his calls and those of the birds. Each spring he conducts an annual bird count, helped by relatives and students; his lifetime list for the region now includes around 200 varieties.

Lee points out damage from spruce budworms, other elements of ecological processes and interrelationships. Kabetogama had been logged, there had been intense fires fueled by the pile-up of slashings; now it is unlikely that the big pines will ever return, or if so, not for hundreds or thousands of years: There is too thin a layer of soil above the rock base. Yet the creation of Voyageurs Park, one of the first major efforts to take land that has been used and attempt to re-establish a wilderness ecosystem, indicates how important it is to the nation as a whole to safeguard some islands of beauty and wilderness amid the intensive, sometimes excessive use of the land. Voyageurs was a long time coming about; it is only a few years old and fancy visitor facilities are off in the future.

We emerge at Locator Lake abruptly, the forest having screened it from view until the trail stops at lakeshore. Stark, high cliffs surround the long, winding lake and David stands silently on the gravel of the beach.

"It's so . . . so beautiful!" says David after a while.

I am surprised; I would have expected a nine-year-old to want to canoe the lake, to explore this remote place. But he stands and stares and drinks it in and I am touched by his sensibility. The stewardship of land brings many rewards.

Tucked in the brush are two motorboats, the motors and gas cans apparently cached and hidden farther away by resort owners who fly visitors in by seaplane. Technically this is not allowed, but the park is new and the park service treads a tender trail of carrying out its legal responsibilities and at the same time not offending any more people than necessary. Flying in fishermen is a longstanding practice and old customs die hard, notwithstanding the large number of good fishing lakes nearby that are outside the park. The last group to have flown in left a residue of tin cans, tinfoil, and debris, which we pick up to pack out on our return hike.

Had there not been a public outcry in behalf of the park, had Voyageurs not been established, David and I and the others would have been greeted by shoreline real estate development and condominiums, for that had been the plan for the area fifteen years ago. But the public interest won and the park came about, breathing hope for the future. Now the quality and the character of the park are being impinged by what seem the most narrow and short-term gains of politicians, and the time has come once again for a rallying, a mustering in behalf of the future if our stewardship of the land for our children and grandchildren is to have meaning.

*   *   *

Back at Kabetogama a blustering wind is whipping the lake into whitecaps. We attempt the crossing and are beaten back by the wind. I fret at exposing David to the danger, though he seems unafraid.

We lounge on the shore, screened by a point of land, dawdling over our lunch, speculating when the wind will abate.

"Save one sandwich and one cup of lemonade, David."

"Why, Dad? I'm hungry."

"We may be sitting here several hours. You'll be more hungry by late afternoon."

He argues, I get stern, he puts the second sandwich aside.

"Do you think there is old Indian pottery around here?" David asks, perpetually the collector.

"I doubt it. Too rocky." The entire region has been inhabited by Indians since the last glacier receded about 12,000 years ago, and park service archeologists have located prehistoric fire rings, campsites, and artifacts.

"Let's go exploring," Lee suggests. We fan out, each on his own bent. I discover an endless growth of wild raspberries and augment lunch, then notice an odd rectangular depression about ten feet by fifteen. Soil and stones had been excavated and birmed, and huge trees have grown atop the foundation. The trees are at least 150 to 200 years old, one of the rare groves of large pines still left, so whatever structure had stood here predated the trees. A crude trapper's shelter? An Indian winter lodge? I call Lee over, and he will have the archeologists check.

Back on shore the whitecaps are rolling, undulating, and it is pointless to even try to canoe. Do we want to be fetched, the ranger motorboat inquires via Lee's walkie-talkie. We look at each other, shrug our shoulders.

"We'll wait a while," Lee answers.

David returns from his safari, trying to look nonchalant.

"Is this anything, Dad?"

He knows perfectly well that it is an Indian spearpoint, the tip broken off. Not just any old spearpoint; shape and flaking suggest that it is very old, possibly prehistoric, which would date its manufacture to about 2,000 to 3,000 years ago. It is found in the park and must perforce be given to the park for its museum, which makes David unhappy.

"We'll put your name on it and the date that you found it," Lee consoles. "It will always be yours, your find, but we will keep it for you so everyone can enjoy it."

As we wait for the storm to pass to canoe back in the usual late afternoon calm, it occurs to me that we are stewards not only of the land, but also of our allotted time. Both are gifts to us, which we did not create. Only our use of them, our respect for them, and our husbandry of them govern the quality of our lives.

We set out finally, despite the continuing wind, which has dropped somewhat. The paddling is difficult as veering gusts come broadside, then quartering. We strain across open water to rest behind an island, then strain once more to reach the next shelter. It is a longer paddle to go island hopping, but safer. David and I paddle hard; I see the others struggling also. Is his life jacket tied? How can I expose him to such risk? What am I doing here, anyway? Worry triggers adrenalin flow; we paddle on, not daring to pause and drift broadside to the waves.

Behind the next island we rest and I tell David, "Now is the time."

"Time for what?"

"For the sandwich and lemonade."

"Tastes good," he munches. "I was really hungry."

*   *   *

The boy has learned much in one brief day. About himself, about the world that spins him through time, about beauty. It came hard to set aside half his lunch as safeguard against later hunger; so perhaps he has learned that a partially sated appetite at midday was sufficient, that the saved food gave him needed energy and strength in late afternoon when he had to make a great effort and it had become necessary that he paddle without missing a stroke.

He discovered that he could exert himself steadily and for long periods of time, beyond routine tiredness, and still function effectively. It is gratifying to test one's strength and stamina and find them adequate. The long hike, the hard canoeing were such tests.

And I learned more about his sensibility and sensitivity, about his unfolding, emerging personality and character, the new butterfly, fresh from its cocoon, spreading its fragile and soft wings in the sun that they may harden and enable it to fly.

*   *   *

It was never guaranteed anywhere, by anyone, that Voyageurs National Park should come into existence. It could as easily have gone the other way, when the battles were being fought between those who sought the establishment of this park and those who wanted to use the land privately, commercially, not necessarily intending ill, but certainly not wishing to safeguard the place so that David's children and theirs in turn would have it to come to as a source of beauty, of environmental integrity, as a permanent bastion of physical, emotional, and spiritual health.

Our society's values about what constitutes the best and the most appropriate use of the land have gone through many changes, and they are unique to the United States. We have come all the way from heedless, reckless exploitation and abuse of the seemingly endless frontier and unlimited resources to one of slowly growing realization that there is a limit, that there can be irreversible damage done.

A century ago we set aside a few places of beauty as parks; it was almost a throw-away since there was so much land. Putting some of it aside did not matter that much overall. We have come now to the point of taking used land and seeking to not only protect it, but to try to re-establish a viable ecosystem while there is still an opportunity to do so. The beneficiaries are to be not only ourselves, but the generations to come after us, that they may have an opportunity, a choice, to enhance their lives with beauty and a healthy outdoors.

Yet there is another change in attitude in the offing, discernible at places such as Voyageurs: It is a wish to do the right thing, tempered by the continuous process of political horse trading to appease local, vested, and financial interests. As a consequence, the parks are becoming legal tender in the electoral process, and decisions are tempered and compromised with a view to their value on the hustings in state legislative districts, in congressional races. Like federal discretionary grants bestowed in return for primary election support and promised support in the final election, so is it seeming to go with policy and management decisions affecting parklands.

Should snowmobiling be allowed? How many snowmobile enthusiasts are there, in which district? With what impact on State Senator X's election? And how much pressure will Congressman Y bring to bear? A decision that ought to be made on the basis of the impact of snowmobile use on the parkland, on the habitat, its wildlife, its human users, is made instead on the basis of the short-term politicians' and bureaucrats' fortunes.

This is a dangerous *non sequitur* in the political process. It is one thing to withhold money for harbor improvements in Chicago because the mayor won't support the presidential candidate; the harbor project can always be funded the next year, or the year after. But decisions about the land can be irreversible, the impact of human and mechanized use beyond remedy. The bestowing and withholding of federal largesse is a perennial political practice; subjecting national parks management and environmental decisions to the political auction is new and it is obscene, and to the detriment of the statutory mission of the park service.

It is potentially to the detriment of the Davids of the world, and their children, and theirs in turn. For if enough bad decisions are made over a long enough period, the harm can be irreversible. And if that happens, if the character and integrity of Voyageurs National Park and other parks are so affected, the future generations will have been robbed of the opportunity, the very ability, to safeguard and enhance the land. We ought not to play petty, temporal politics with the perishable, delicate webwork that is the quality of life on the land.

David's day in the park was a priceless gift to him from the land, and from the countless people who cared enough to give of themselves to create this park. Whether David's children and grandchildren will have an equal opportunity for such experiences depends on us, on the commitment we are willing to make, the effort we are willing to put forth, the love of the land we are willing to put into action.

The issue at stake is Voyageurs and every other national park now in existence, and those that may yet come to be. That ten, twenty, two hundred years from now a youngster can come

out upon Locator Lake and pause, and say, "It's so . . . so beautiful."

The issue is respect for Creation.

24 Fringed Gentian Returns to a Ravaged Land

Connotations are such private, personal matters. The sight of the orange-yellow school bus reminds one of my neighbors of his boyhood, riding his horse eleven miles to high school in town, because when he had completed country elementary school, there was no public transportation. He rode his horse in mild weather, and hiked there and back when he could not ride. This was in addition to the farm chores, the early milking, the feeding, the cleaning of the barn. He wanted an education very much and was willing to make the effort; his children, now grown, rode the bright-colored buses to school.

"It reminds me of my third grade teacher," someone else says. "Was she ever strict. . . . "

"Reminds me of the day the bus broke down at the S-curve, thirty below zero and a howling wind and the driver says ____ "

Same bus, different connotations and remembrances.

*   *   *

There comes a day in late summer, usually after a rain the evening before, when the fringed gentian erupt into bloom. It is a most beautiful wildflower, a biennial gift of nature. The blooms are deep purple, four petals edged in a delicate fringe. The purple petals unfold gently, spread to the warming sun, then twist together and enfold each other in cooling evening, until by nightfall they have become invisible, the tight purple twists seemingly regressing into the green stems. They have become invisible, difficult to locate, and are thus in early morn-

117

ing. As sunlight warms, they unclasp again and become bold flags in the late summer meadowland.

When the fringed gentian appears, it is a signal that summer is at fruition, about to turn to autumn. The nights will cool now, the days still warm—sometimes. Then, unexpectedly, the days are cool: overcast, blustery, only to turn warm again. There is a coquettish cast to the weather, a teasing to it, that travels parallel to the opening and closing of the flower during its time of bloom. Overhead the birds that will migrate begin to gather, not quite done with their molting. It is a time of resumption of school, of preparing for fall, of garnering fuel and food for winter.

*   *   *

The first gentian bloomed on the tree farm almost ten years after the pine plantation had been put in. The one-time fields had not been plowed for a number of years, deserted and fallow. Then the trees had been planted, tiny and slow to grow after the shock of transfer from nursery seedbed to farmfield. Only then did the gentian return to the lowland, the moist little islands. It is as though the trees gave way there, allowing open spots, so that the flowers would have a place to grow, the selfish giants opening their arms that the children might play.

My father, alive then and visiting, was the first to notice the gentian, and look as we might, we found only one. Where had it come from? Seed deposited by a bird? Some plants hiding, harboring in secret nooks and hidden spots, and suddenly spreading in a more hospitable setting? The wildflowers do hide in secret places, tiny, rare orchids where you would least expect: trailing arbutus amid some princess pine.

"They grow in the Alps," Father said. "I remember them there."

He had been a climber in his youth, a hiker in middle age. Then he was advancing in years; the lovely flower had opened to warm him with the memories stored long in his mind.

The single bloom was not followed by another the next year, but the year after that there were a half dozen. Then more.

Now they show each August or September, ever spreading where moisture and meadow invite them.

"The mountain people in the Tirol and Switzerland make medicine from the roots," Father recollected. "And a kind of brandy."

"Yes." I recalled it very well, a youngster in Europe, being administered bitter dosages of the concoction for various intestinal and stomach upsets. The cure seemed definitely worse than the disease and led me to sympathize with Tom Sawyer when his Aunt Polly was forever administering evil-tasting nostrums to him.

The whole genus *Gentiana*, comprising about 400 species, is named for the Illyrian king Gentius, who supposedly discovered the medicinal value of the root, a bit of knowledge I could have done without. I hated the bitter taste of the stuff as a child, and while my father remembered the beauty of the flowers in Alpine meadows, I remembered that the grizzled old-timer who furnished the gentian brandy on our annual mountain climbing outings died from drinking the stuff. This did not surprise me, though it shocked my parents and ended the presence of it from the family pharmacopoeia.

"But it was so effective," Mother said sadly, dumping the remaining supply down the drain.

"I hear he was snowbound," Dad said, "and drank up his remaining supply. When it was gone, he ate the roots at the bottom of the jug. They found him dead after the snowstorm."

The tough, flexible root rarely branches. It is brown and spongy, tastes bitter. The bitterness comes from the glucoside, soluble in water and alcohol. However, the gentian roots are almost identical to that of hellebore, a poisonous plant. Perhaps the old-folk medicine man of the Tirolean mountains had picked some hellebore with the gentian. Picked, pickled, partied, and packed it in. So long as I did not have to ingest the concoction, I could appreciate the beauty of the flowers. Dad's approach to gentian was entirely aesthetic, but then he never had to take the elixir.

*   *   *

119

This year the gentian can no longer be counted. It has become generic to the reburgeoning land. It grows along the creekbank now as well as in the meadows. Its bright purple is intermixed with the bold yellow of goldenrod, the lilac of asters, the white of daisies. It is a strong witness to the ability of nature, given a chance, to reassert itself in its diversity and beauty, an expression of ecological vitality.

And it is a symbol to me also of the end of the growing season, the terminus of summer. The land flies a purple flag heralding the beginning, when in spring the swamp iris and the crocus bloom. It flies the purple flag heralding the end with the fringed purple gentian. I hope it blooms another day, another week, perhaps even a month. For when the gentian is gone the frost will have come.

25 Intimations of Mortality

Some birds are already winging through on their migration south, for in the arctic nesting grounds the summer has already died. Here the weather patterns are gradually veering to the cool side, give or take a warm afternoon here, a not-so-cold night there. Oh yes, there will be warm spells, even an Indian summer if we are fortunate, though there have been years when that delightful interlude has passed us by and we have gone from the cool to the clammy to the cold.

Local flocks of birds are preparing for the migration, gathering on an evening to try the communal sport of constituting a crowd. It seems disorderly when the blackbirds try it, the total absence of formation or pattern contrasting to the precision of the geese when they ultimately come. The blue jays, who winter here, already sound more raucous and assertive, as though looking forward to having more of the turf to themselves. The other evening, sitting quietly beneath a pine at dusk, I observed a blue jay scolding a big deer passing beneath his tree. And the buck stands, listens, then snorts once, twice. An unlikely bit of communication.

Leaves are turning, of course, even the older twin needles of the Norway pine turning orange and then brown. The season of growth has come to an end. Soon the world will be sere and dormant, preparing for winter—which has a life all its own. It is a different world then, a different expression of existence.

*   *   *

It is said that as we grow older, then old, our thoughts and attitudes about dying change. Ultimately we accept the inevitability, and then the imminence of death. We no longer fret and worry about whether it will be; instead we become concerned about the moment of it: Will it be accompanied by pain? Will we be alone? Will someone be with us? Who will it be, a friend, a loving person, a relative? Or will we pass into oblivion in desolation, crossing the threshold in utter aloneness?

The death of the old harlot in the motion picture *Zorba the Greek* contains an ideal of dying with love. Through the waning years of her life she is growing ever-more unattractive and consequently more assertive about her one-time beauty and desirability. Now she is on her deathbed. In the anteroom the vultures wait, the village harridans anxious for her last breath so that they might ransack the woman's belongings, rifle the paltry few clothes and knickknacks. But she is not yet dead, not quite, and Zorba is by her bedside, holding her hand. Yes, he assures her, she is the loveliest of women, the most desirable. Yes, he loves her above all others. And yes, she smiles as she expires. That the greedy people then instantly descend on the deathroom and rob it, scurrying about like rats, no longer matters to her; it is a reflection only on them. For the harlot died reassured of love, the passage eased, her hand held. It was a loving death. She died, Zorba reinforcing her pitiful illusions; does that matter? Much of our life view of ourselves and our function in the world is illusory and phantasmic, and if the reality contains a small measure of shared love and kindness, well, what better companions could there be at the end?

*　　　*　　　*

The changing of the seasons that culminates now, testifying through the migrations of birds, through the preparation of dormancy by some animals (the striped gophers have already gone underground!), the turning of leaf colors and then their cascading to the ground—all this has a lack of tenderness. Closure and termination, the beginning of the end, are very unlike the spring with its connotation of growth and new life and therefore of love.

Yet is it necessarily so that it must be likewise with humans?

Some years ago it fell to me to nurse my first wife's grandfather in his terminal illness. He was by then a tiny whipcord of a man in his nineties, a sinewy Scandinavian said to have been the first settler's child born in Freeborn County, an insurance man, paterfamiliar, good humored in a quiet, awe-inspiring manner. But now he was weakening perceptibly, rarely speaking from his hospital bed, but smiling when I wiped his face, spoke to him, held his hand. Always doughty and feisty, he came to a point when he wanted to die. He waved off the suction tube that assisted his breathing with a feeble gesture, and he clasped my hand as his breath became more labored, slower, the respirations shallower, coming at longer intervals, then ceasing.

It was the moment of giving up the will, the desire to live, that was particularly poignant. It was such a deliberate, cognitive decision, a saying of "I have had enough and do not wish to go on any more; I am tired beyond resuscitation and desire nothing more than to rest." Sweet sleep. Blessed necromancer.

*   *   *

It is the giving up of the will to live that presents the problem to me when the semiannual malaise is upon me. Both at spring breakup, when I find myself physically isolated in a hostile environment, mired in mud and receding snow, and now, it is easy for me to consider death as preferable to the effort of living.

The experience and the knowledge gained from living through the ending of many summers provide me no succor when this desolation is upon me. Even the humor and the whimsy of the exchange between blue jay and deer bring at most a wry, faint smile of brief duration. My mind tells me that the falling leaves will insulate and eventually nourish the trailing arbutus that erupts with the next spring; it does not impact the melancholy.

I know that the death of a season is not the end of the world, merely a necessary and inevitable phase of the continuum of nature and of life. I know that this irrevocable termination of another year's growing is only faintly related to my own ultimate death. I know all this, but I do not feel it. This gap, this inter-ruption of synapse between knowing something and feeling it, is the area of the spirit, of one's internal spiritual life. It is an element of existence nourished by human love and relation-ships, by the phenomena of nature and the world, by the arts and beauty, by work and avocations; all those failing, there are of course one's beliefs and prayer.

We can be reasonably sure that day follows night; it is just a little bit hard sometimes to believe it and to want it to be so.

26 Step Gently Unto the Good Land

Tony transplants small spruce trees from the woods to border his patch of garden, gerrymandered in the middle of the family plot. He spaces them a few inches apart, stands back to admire his work.

"Seedbed?" I ask.

"Fence to keep out the dog and the twins."

It won't work. Should I tell him?

"It won't work. And it's right in the middle of the garden, where I have to till."

Tony looks unhappy, but there is something about his posture that says he will not move those trees. I should not have poured cold water on his project; he worked steadfastly for several hours, careful to dig out the trees with balls of dirt around the roots, hauling them a good distance to the garden. I am an insensitive parent.

Tony is busily watering his transplants just as I begin the rototilling, wrestling with the awkward machine, fussing at my wife for picking such a downhill-uphill plot and at Tony for putting the obstacle square in the middle of it, then compounding my difficulties by watering the entire region just as I set out to till it.

He is eleven and mercurial, a facet of the age. Busy with dreams and fantasies, with play and pestering David.

"Here's a poem I wrote," he says.

It starts as doggerel and ends as free verse, deploring littering and pollution, warning the world against becoming a wasteland. All bang and no whimper. Now he is walking up the driveway with a garbage bag on his way to the county road to pick up tin cans and trash thrown out the windows of passing cars. On his way he kicks David's ball into the tall grass, and as he rounds the corner I notice his jacket on the ground, my best axe near the cornpatch, and his bicycle in the driveway.

* * *

The garden thrives through the summer. The dog is disinterested and the twins are kept out by threats of manslaughter, their mother's long arms, and everyone's efforts at distraction.

Tony is again watering his spruce seedlings. With fastidious attention bestowed on them, the little trees are candling and growing. His vegetables are doing better than the rest of the family's.

"It's the trees," he claims. "Keeps out the dog and the twins. Also it's putting something back in the earth."

I suspect it is the daily watering, but this time I hold my tongue although I am still smarting from having to till circles around his plot.

* * *

The notion that you have to give something to get something is intriguing. But is life a horse trade? A matter of buying, of even embezzling your way into heaven? Or does one do good for its own sake and value only, expecting nothing in return?

Some years ago we were hunting moose far north of here in Canada, north even of the Hudson Bay railroad tracks. A friend who is a very traditional Indian and I canoed into the back country, camped, and hunted. A nonsmoker who disapproved of my nicotine habit, I was surprised one morning when he asked for one of my cigarettes. He walked off with the cigarette unlit.

Later that day we did see a moose. My companion fired, but the bullet was deflected by brush. Sitting around a small cookfire that evening he mused about it.

"It wasn't right. I expected something in return for the offering. I should have offered something to show that I was willing to enter into the spirit of life and creation. . . . It doesn't work any other way."

It is this willingness to accept life and creation as one finds it that appears to me to be the key to a satisfactory relationship with one's existence. The little tokens we offer, whether tobacco, donations, good deeds, or spruce trees, are no more and no less than expressions of our acceptance of something greater than ourselves. These are not actions for which we will be rewarded by anyone else; by expecting such a reward we are due for disappointment. The reward comes from within ourselves and stems from the human spirit's willingness to accept life. This I believe to be the meaning of an offering.

*   *   *

I get mixed signals from Tony. One moment he is a heedless youngster, the next a deeply sensitive person concerned about the quality of the environment, and wants to become a naturalist.

The mornings are frosty now, the white sheathing of the grass and remaining leaves thawing under the midday sun, only to reappear the next morning. Overhead the ducks and geese are migrating, and the smaller birds come through in scattered little flocks. It is a time when the air, the sky combine to etch the outlines of trees clearly, when outdoor silhouettes are remarkably clean. When the colors are changing kaleidoscopically, like refracted light dancing on a marble floor.

The garden is done and prepared for tilling, a mountain of compost and organic matter waiting to be spread before the soil is turned. Next spring, after the accumulation of snow with its heavy nitrogen content, the plot will be plowed again before planting.

"You can rototill the garden now," Tony informs me. "I've pulled all my plants. Ate the last of the beets last night."

I know that without being told; he let them cook too long and the burning odor penetrated the house, but I say nothing.

"You won't have to go in circles with the rototiller, either," Tony goes on. "It'll be easier just going in straight rows."

"What did you do with the spruce?"

"I'll show you."

He leads me down the driveway to the little waiting house we are building for those cold mornings when he and David have to wait for the school bus. The structure is made of old logs, salvaged from a log house being torn down.

All about the waiting house are Tony's little spruce. They have been planted, mulched, watered. They are at eight-feet intervals, well tamped and set.

"They'll make a good windbreak here, and a snowbreak," Tony explains. "About the time Micah and Megan go to school and wait for the bus, the trees will be a nice size."

"Beautiful, a really beautiful piece of work."

We inspect the little planting closely.

"Do you want some caragana shoots? Siberian pea?"

"Oh yes, the birds come to eat the seeds."

"We'll dig them out across the road this weekend. That'll look nice."

In springtime hummingbirds feed on the caragana blooms, in fall the migrating birds seek the seeds from the pealike pods.

"The trees will be big before I finish school," Tony muses.

"And maybe they will be very big when your children go to school," I add.

"I was thinking about that," he says.

As we walk home I have the impression that Tony planted the trees as an offering, enjoying the doing of it, the giving of the gift, and that the expectation of reward is remote, unimportant to him. He is growing up, maturing.

27 How Much Do You See When the Leaves Fall?

Walking in the woods on an autumn day, the colors are intense and vibrant. Green pine contrasts with yellow aspen, red maple, and scarlet flashes from the oaks. The tamarack, or larch, is golden yellow of iridescent brilliance against the blue sky. Already the ground is carpeted with shed pine needles and leaves, moist from dew and beginning to decompose. The faint acrid odor signals the process. It is a silent time to be in the forest, the footfalls swallowed, thus emphasizing even further the visual challenge.

Then there comes a day when enough leaves have dropped to unveil the woods. One sees farther, deeper into the configuration of trees and brush. The curtained screen is going, gone. What was a rustle before is a partridge now, walking, craning its neck to peer at danger; or a red squirrel interring pine cones and acorns; a young deer still learning to be cautious; a cluster of chickadees flitting about. The sounds are no longer disembodied and subject to speculation, but lend themselves to observation. The workings of the forest are no longer quite such a mystery.

Some years this phenomenon is more vivid than others, depending on ground moisture and temperature cycles. This is a banner year, memorable in the lifetime collection of autumns, leaving a sharp imprint among the stored data in the mind.

*   *   *

In some respects we, as human beings, are like the forest in autumn. We grow our own screening foliage through our lives, accumulating defensive screens supposed to obstruct the peering gaze of intruders.

"No, didn't bother me a bit," I reply to an acquaintance's question about my boyhood experiences as a refugee, fleeing from the Nazis while most of my family was dragnetted to extermination camps. "We got out safely."

I do not want to relive the pain and the fear, the trauma of losing my sense of who I was and where, in all creation, was my little corner of turf, my place of belonging. I deny it happened, that it hurt; deny it to others and thereby to myself. Screening leaves designed to let me breathe and live without fear or pain. Though the trouble with such defensive structures is that they often do not work. My denial does not affect the questioner, it only obscures and suppresses my own feelings and thoughts.

The truth is that only by admitting that it hurt, that it injured and scarred me, can I be rid of it, or at least move the event from the category of perpetual discomfort to something I can accept as having happened and now being done and over.

The leaves did not fall from this particular ghost in my life until the television series of "Holocaust" some years ago. Since I had been unable to communicate my own experiences to my children, I thought they might learn something about this bit of family history by watching the show. It soon became apparent that it was very disturbing, even in its sanitized video version interspersed incongruously with commercials.

"Was it really like that?" Tony asks as I drift into the bedroom where he, David, and my wife are huddled among pillows.

I join them for a while, am drawn into the show by their further questions and their need for answers. We sit crowded together, huddled.

"It was like that, Tony. Only dirtier, shabbier, and there was more hate, much more hate."

The children's need to know blew away the lifelong screen I had held around me, like an autumn gust of wind whipping away the leaves, and I let down the barriers and let them see me and know me, and came to know myself in the process.

It is ironic that Tony would be the one to break my shell, for he is particularly prone to be uncommunicative about things that bother him. A fight at school? No. Problem with the teacher? No. Tiff with your best friend? No. Hungry? No. Later, much later, sometimes days and weeks later, the truth emerges. He feels bad, rejected, unloved, unlovable, because his best friend does not answer his letters.

David tends to be more forthright and direct, sometimes aggressively so. And while they are young, the twins seem quite different from each other in this regard. Megan, like David, gives voice immediately and loudly. Micah appears more inward.

"Does something hurt?"

"No." Loud weeping.

"Micah, does your tummy hurt?"

"No." Louder wailing.

"Your throat? Ears?"

"No no no no no."

But he tugs at his ears and it turns out to be a painful middle-ear infection. Only on the way home from the doctor's does he say it:

"Ears hurt."

Denying it did not make the pain go away.

* * *

With each passing day I can see farther into the forest. I know every hill and undulation in the lay of my land and yet each growing season, as the leaves, brush, and grasses mask the view, it assumes an impenetrability and consequently an air of mystery. Even though I know what is behind the screen. It is the aura of mystery that is the illusion, for the reality has been, is, and will be there and I am familiar with it.

The reality of human conflict, pain, and hurt seems to have been a quintessential component of life since time immemorial. Humankind has distilled the worst and the most commonplace of these into myths and parables. Oedipus, Noah, Clytemnestra, Job . . . Medea, Perseus. In every culture, civilization, and language. Nanabosho stories and legends of the Wendigo.

Their universal purpose is to tell us that others have suffered what we have, have committed the evils and harms that we have, have been victimized as we have. It is a sharing of the human condition and experience in distilled form.

And yet we find it hard at times to admit our humanity, our capacity for hurt and for fear. We prefer to hide ourselves behind defenses that fool only ourselves and we refuse to apply to ourselves the lessons learned so painfully by those who have been there before us. The forest is still there, the individual trees and outcroppings and the dips and valleys in the land, however many leaves may mask them.

In the autumn of life more of these leaves fall and drop. Under the impact of intimacy, of love, and of trust in relationships, I unmask, as does nature.

28 Ducks are Limited, Clucks Unlimited

Foggy. Water warmer than air. Wisps and tendrils of whitish-gray keep rising from the water, meeting the vapor of the low cloud cover. I hike the half mile to the river, lugging waders, decoys, shotgun, and high expectations. I forego my blind on the bank and wade to the waterlogged island where I quickly makeshift another, then set out the decoys.

I have no inclination to go on safari, to drive many miles and stay at motels or at campgrounds, just because the calendar and the conservation department declare the opening of season. I would sooner go near my home when the weather is right, when the flights are on, and when I feel like it. In my island blind now, nursing a steaming cup of coffee while looking down at the shin-deep water, I listen for the calls of ducks or geese overhead, for the sound of wingbeats.

"Quaaaack . . . quaaaack. . . ." I call, trying to make it sound alluring, inviting. Never successful with storebought calls, I have come to rely on my own voice.

Without warning a mallard splashes down among the decoys, then another. I am ready for the next and the ones after. A good morning's hunt. A bit of work, some effort to retrieve in the shallow river. I am cautious about the potholes; some years past I stepped into one, my waders filling up in the deep, and it had been a struggle to get free.

The fog burns off after lunch, ending the hunting.

*   *   *

The memory of the long-ago hunt is still pleasant, though I

stopped shooting ducks many years ago. There are not all that many. I don't feel right about it when the number of ducks has declined. Geese don't breed hereabouts and rarely land during migration.

With the advent of the season our land is posted, the flag hoisted to the top of the pole so as to clearly mark the location of our residence, and I deliver the annual warning.

"Always wear red," I admonish the children. "That creek in front of the place . . . the little lake . . . who knows. . . ."

"Nobody would be dumb enough to hunt there," David scoffs. "They'd sink out of sight in the silt."

"It's like quicksand," says Tony.

They ought to know. They've been warned repeatedly to stay away, that one cannot ever try to walk out of the deep morass but must crayfish, must crawl out. Of course they had to try it. Abashed, they rinsed their mudcaked clothes in the creek, and I saw them spread over bushes to dry.

"Wear something red anyhow. You never know about these damn fools."

Nearby gunfire startles us. I am torn between flattening the children on the floor and lying on top of them, and hastening outside to see who is shooting at what, and from where. I go out.

A blue pickup is parked on the dirt road bluff overlooking the little pond, across the water from our house. A hunter is in the cab, shooting out of the window at a couple of bluebills in the middle of the lake.

"How would he have gotten the ducks if he had been able to hit them?" Tony wants to know.

"Maybe they've got a dog in the camper," David theorizes. The camper is a glistening contraption, surely outfitted with every convenience, perhaps including a retriever.

The truck disappears in a cloud of dust.

"Wear red!" I command.

*   *   *

A school day, older children safely in town. A knock on the

door. This hunter is splendidly dressed, straight Abercrombie and Fitch, except for the mud dripping from knees down.

"Could I use your phone? My car is stuck just down the road a little."

The roads are dry and I can't imagine where one would mire.

"There is this little tote road just the other side of this lake," he explains.

I know it well. It has been flooded for years, is in disuse, overgrown, and blocked by a barricade and boulders, and a shrill NO TRESPASSING — NO HUNTING sign in Day-Glo colors, which I put there to keep out the unwary, not to mention safeguarding the children's lives.

"I didn't see those rocks," he says, not mentioning the sign.

The car teeters on the rocks. If the children were home they would claim it for a teeter-totter. A neighbor with a tractor, jacks, planks, and chains comes to the rescue and charges accordingly.

*　　　*　　　*

The middle of the pond draws a handful of migrating ducks daily. They are unhuntable, having a good view all around and out of range of everything except field artillery and hand grenades. There is no safe place for a blind in the quagmire surrounding the water.

Indian summer is at its prime. Gunfire nearby, followed by loud shouts, curses. Another pickup truck is parked by the road. A small duckboat with two men and a dog are in the lake. One man is pointing, tugging at the collar of the reluctant Chesapeake.

"Get in there and retrieve, you useless. . . ."

The dog braces his legs against the sides of the craft. The owner picks up the dog and throws him in the water.

"Now fetch, dammit!"

Somehow they have managed to shoot a duck. The dog paddles toward it, mouths it, and swims toward the opposite shore where I am standing. He deposits the duck at my feet, near the doorstep, wags his tail. It is a merganser, a diving duck, not very good to eat.

"Oh, I didn't see your house," a hunter calls from the boat.

"You didn't see the signs either."

"Sorry. Here mutt."

I hope he is talking to the dog. The retriever looks at me, back to his owner, then reluctantly heads back to the lakeshore and stops. He sniffs the marshy ooze and sits down.

"Come!"

The dog sits.

"Come!" Lending emphasis, the hunter stands and bellows again: "Come here!"

The little boat tips over and they swim, pushing it to shore. Dog and I watch with interest. About fifteen feet out they make contact with the silt bottom. As they try to stand and shove the boat, they sink. The mud gives off gurgles.

"Hey, Tony and David, come out here."

"This is better than cartoons on television," says David, joining me. Soon we are all sitting on the grass enjoying the show. Micah and Megan clamor to go swimming too, and the hunters glare at them. There is no way for the hunters to walk, no longer any way to swim in the muck. They must dogpaddle through the silt, pushing the boat every few inches. The retriever decides departure preferable to waiting for the inevitable and trots up the driveway toward the parked truck just as the hunters emerge on land, dragging their duckboat. They leave, carrying the craft.

"Hey mister, you forgot your duck," Tony calls after them, bearing the inedible.

Ducks should be protected, and an open season declared on Clucks Unlimited.

29 The Road to Damascus by Way of the Northwoods

Now that the leaves have fallen, the tamarack needles have shed, the in-flight clucking of the pileated woodpeckers is clearly audible. Sounds carry more distinctly and travel farther, and the gradual cooling compels the large, flamboyantly crested birds to forage more vigorously. They must alter feeding territories and readjust turf commensurate with the cyclical change in ecosystem balances. Different foods must be found, and in different places. They come closer to the house now, occasionally into the yard to feast on suet when it gets really cold.

Being cognizant of the little things about me has become more than habit. It is a necessity.

I do not live through the day listening for the pileated, but when he clucks I hear it, know what it is, and make mental note of it, for something lovely has happened, something that enriches the day. Whether it is this birdsound, or the call of a loon overhead, or some particular coloring or pattern of the lake, a colorcast of the tamarack, there is usually some aspect of the world and the life in it that adds beauty to my partaking. For I have learned that my own life is a gift over which I exercise no ownership. I am not the proprietor of my time of life, merely the custodian, guardian, the steward. The extent and quality of my appreciation for other aspects of this same phenomenon enhances my respect for my own.

*   *   *

This perception became clearer to me over the years and gradually so, until a most unlikely encounter in an unexpected

137

place. My personal road to Damascus was by way of the Air and Space Museum in Washington, and it has led me to live out my life in the northwoods with greater cognition.

Air and Space is a marvelous museum. It is so large that it requires many visits, so complex, yet so intelligently planned and designed that all ages find things of interest and value, and come from it having learned and enjoyed. At the end of a visit, the children satiated and tired, we pass the entrance to a side gallery I had overlooked previously: Is there life in space? Come on a simulated voyage into the universe!

I purchase a snack for the children and bid them wait while I yield to the invitation. Inside the dark gallery, I am quickly enveloped by the sensation of space travel. I am surrounded by screens that display stars, whole planetary systems, traveling past at incredible speeds. Faster and faster and farther I spin from earth, until the illusion is complete and I am speeding through our own system, through the Milky Way, and on.

The sparkling band of stars, which is the Milky Way seen from earth, is a vast conglomerate of complex galaxies. Then even this recedes into distance and becomes a small twinkle in my journey to the far reaches of humankind's present extent of knowledge.

"Let us return to earth now," the commentator announces.

Our imaginary spaceship turns, we retrace our voyage. Speed accelerates, earth looms, becomes larger, the continents discernible. The United States. Florida. A city, a backyard where a man reclines in a lounge chair. The voyage continues! To the skin, a cell of that skin, into the construction of one carbon atom within that cell.

The one atom is as complex, as full of unfathomables and infinities, as that grand space where I had just been. The program ends and I leave the gallery having partaken of an experience that to me borders on the mystic. A single atom within my body is fully as profound as the grandiosity of stellar space. I might not be able to comprehend infinity or eternity; I might not understand the scientific nuances and implications that others, better trained than I, might derive. But I know that there exists a body of knowledge beyond my comprehension, and beyond that knowledge, the unfathomable that will never be within my grasp, and perhaps never within the grasp of any human.

How do I come to be here, in this vast macrocosm? I am a being whose microscopic makeup is a complex miracle, and I find myself in a universe that is just as complex, just as unknowable. Who, what am I? The product of countless generations, of a veritable chain of lives stretching far back into time? But this being that is "I" also reaches forward into time, through my children, into existence that is as unknowable to me as is the lifechain that produced me. I can know no more of the lifechain of which I am a part, of the future, than I know of my own past. For try as I might, I can reconstruct my ancestry only fragmentally, one branch to the year 1400 A.D., another to the middle 1800s; of others I know nothing, and all of it is but a speck of time considering how long this chain has been.

It is the same with my daily life; however, I complicate it through petty, unrealistic wants and desires. I might actually know and understand only portions of it. The least I can do is to accept my limits of knowledge and of intellect and appreciate the whole of the gift that is my life, understanding of it only portions.

*　　　*　　　*

I am hunting in the woods, walking silently in the wind blusters and gusts of sleet, uphill and into the wind. Topping the crest, I sit at the foot of a large Norway pine to rest, to peer down among the trees and into the marsh, hoping a deer will emerge, for in weather like this they sometimes bed down on the windy side of a hill, part way up, where scents will most likely come to them.

My ears acclimate to the sounds of wind, creaking branches, the few remaining sere leaves. I hear an occasional crackle of breaking branches below me. A deer, I think. Perhaps a small one. I watch, peer, see nothing, but continue to hear. After about fifteen minutes of this intermittent sound, the animal emerges. It is a timber wolf hunting mice, crisscrossing below me, its nose near the ground. The animal is in prime, the winterpelt full around the neck, shoulders, and chest; the hind half has a faintly rufous tinge. The tail is full, tipped white. The wolf's hunt is fruitless and it starts up the hill toward me, following the deer runway I have been watching. Nose to the ground, it comes closer, to thirty feet, then twenty, when it notices me and stops, looks, and we peer into one another's eyes. The wolf turns then, trots back down the hill where it stops again to look at me: Once again I get a full, clear view of the face, the front, then profile and sideview as it turns to the marsh to continue the hunt. I can see it for several minutes more, hear it longer, before both sight and sound exceed my ability to perceive, just as was the case with my voyage into the universe, with my endeavors to comprehend my own past and my future.

I can know only relatively little, but I can appreciate the beauty and the marvel of the here and now, of the great loan granted to me which I call life, which I am to steward as I steward the land.

30 My Dear Hunter

"Tomorrow," says Peggy, "we have a babysitter and we can both go deer hunting."

We like to hunt quietly, meandering through the woods, standing, walking softly, mindful of the wind and the way the deer tend to travel.

"I'll go around the spruce hill and skirt the swamp. . . . Come out just past the white pine hit by lightning."

"Give me a few minutes to mosey around. I'll be waiting up that hill, where the red-tailed hawk had her nest. Ten minutes."

Then there are times when we are off in different directions by mutual consent, hunting privately. A very comfortable way of doing things that suits our preferences. But it does not work all of the time. This year seems to have been jinxed.

"Where were you?" I ask her back at the house. "I cut through the tagalder swamp and across the ridge and came out right where you said you'd be!"

I am miffed, having been stood up, having made the arduous walk for naught. One never surprises a deer going through that swamp, it is too noisy. The only time I've seen a deer there was when a group of does about ran me down, being chased by an amorous buck, and that was a few years ago and proved to be an experience that was one of a kind.

"I got cold. And hungry," she says.

"You came in the house with shoes on," Tony upbraids me.

"Five sticks of wood, Dad," David adds. It is the standard penalty.

"I made that long drive all for nothing," I protest. "Five deer could have walked right past your stand."

In fact I had seen no fresh tracks when I came out, but righteous indignation is sufficient grounds for a little prevarication.

"You've got to bring in five sticks of firewood," Tony insists. The customary ingress for family members is through the mud room, where one changes to slippers, and thence into the main part of the house.

Peggy is avoiding my glare, pretending great interest in the steaming bowl of soup and the daily newspaper.

*   *   *

"You mean you haven't seen even one?" she asks several days later, the deer season nearing its end. "All that time out in the woods and you haven't seen even one?" There is an aura of complaint, of fault-finding in her tone of voice. She is begrudging me the time in the woods while she has to go to town to work.

"You can use my rifle and try your luck," I tell her.

"I will," she says, still a bit harsh, belligerent.

She bundles, wraps, bundles up some more, my sylphlike spouse looking like a candidate for Weight Watchers as she rolls out the door.

"That rifle of yours weighs a ton," she complains. "It's a blunderbuss, a cannon."

"Blundercuss, blundercuss," says Megan and Micah echoes her, in love with the sound of the word as Peggy disappears among the trees and I am left watching the children. It is a perfect day for the kind of hunting we like. Not too terribly cold, but the wind is gusting and there is a flurry of alternating sleet and snow in the air. Good for tracking, for silent travel. I am envious, not discouraged at all by five days of failure. But I wish I were going out instead of Peggy as the twins clamor and Tony and David engage in another of their endless disputes.

"Well?" I ask hours later as Peggy returns.

"Well what?" she snaps.

"Did you at least see one?"

"I stepped on one."

"You did what?"

"Big doe. I was following the main runway below the crest of the long hill and I thought that lump forty feet down looked like ears. But it just couldn't be a deer sleeping right in the path, I thought. So I kept going. It was sleeting awfully hard. I looked again and thought it looked suspiciously like a sleeping deer, but who ever heard of one sleeping with you so close. Then when I stepped over the fallen jackpine, it stood up. My, it was big."

"Did you shoot? Did you hit it?"

There is a long silence. "I couldn't get the safety off," she finally says. "That is an awful gun. I don't see how you put up with it all these years."

*   *   *

It is the last weekend of the season. I still have seen nothing.

"But you've been out there from daybreak to nightfall," Peggy reminds me, the complaint evident in her voice.

"Aaarrrgh."

"Daddy said aaarrrgh," Micah points out. "Aaarrrgh."

Peggy and I team up. A lovely early winter day, brisk, windy, not too cold, with a trace of snow on the ground. A few minutes into the forest there are tracks all around. Several deer have been feeding during the night and are probably bedded nearby. We split, agree to rendezvous a few minutes later at the opposite end of the ridge, each of us taking one side of the hill.

I see lots of deer signs on the way but no deer. Peggy is waiting for me at the end of the walk.

"A big buck was watching me as I came over the top," she says. "He just trotted away, I couldn't get a shot at him."

What can I say? We agree she will circle and take a stand nearly half a mile away on the next hill, overlooking the brushy marsh. I will circle the other way, walking fairly slowly but not too quietly. Deer will usually stay up to a quarter mile ahead, and the plan is for me to drive them toward Peggy.

"You've got ten minutes' head start," I say as we part.

It is a fairly hard walk that I take, but I know the terrain well. Shortly before meeting Peggy I hear her shoot, then again. I freeze, listen, wait, give her a few minutes, then go to meet her.

"Two," she says, breathing hard.

"Where are they?" I glance about for the carcasses.

"I don't know. The buck came walking out and I shot, so he stopped and stood there. Then the gun jammed. Then I shot again and he walked about ten feet and disappeared."

We search but there is no blood, no sign of a hit, just footprints of two deer running fast.

We agree to go our separate ways.

*   *   *

The season ends for me as it has gone throughout. I see nothing. Peggy avoids my eyes as she comes in.

"Saw another one," she finally admits. "I was climbing the fence over by the northwest corner and it got up."

"How far away?" I'm not sure I even want to hear this.

"About ten feet."

"Why didn't you shoot?"

"I'd leaned the gun against the fencepost."

*   *   *

"We'll be eating venison after all," I announce two days later.

"But Dad, the season is over!" says David.

"Got one on the way into town this morning."

They are amazed: Daddy is a poacher; my husband, the criminal.

I enjoy being taciturn, munching my supper. Then I relent: "It ran into the side of the truck. I called the game warden and he gave me a permit to keep it."

31 Missed Opportunities, Future Choices

The snow is falling densely in the first major, serious blanketing of the year. A mound, a pyramid, is being built atop the picnic table. Footprints and tiretracks made earlier in the morning have been quickly covered and the flakes are still cascading.

My docket is overfull with pressing chores and long-delayed obligations. Yet I leave it all. This is a moment to put on skis and to relish life. There have been too many missed opportunities; I let things go, put them off, intend to do them later, and the opportunity does not recur. Skiing in the first real snow of winter this year will not be one of them.

The appropriate repartee comes to me too late sometimes. I think of it when the moment is long past. Such an instant came and went last week at Thanksgiving.

David had started my chain of thought the night before with a chance comment about the pilgrims. We were returning from town, the car laden with the last-minute grocery shopping we should have done long before.

"Forget about the fairy tale of the pilgrims for just a minute," I answer David. "All people, everywhere in the world and as far back as history is written or told have celebrated at this time."

"Giving thanks for the harvest?"

"Yes."

"Like Mom opening the pantry and looking at the rows of jars."

Peggy does it when she thinks no one is observing, feasting her eyes on the products of the garden, the fruit jars, the jams and jellies, with a rapt expression. It is a moment of reward, of thankfulness and appreciation, of comfort. I feel good passing the canister of wild rice, and give it a pat. Or the freezer, knowing we have put up meat and vegetables there. Or walking past the woodpile and seeing the winter's supply sawed, split, and stacked.

*　　　*　　　*

There are twenty-three of us for the feast. The children are cheek-by-jowl around the kitchen table, backed by the wood cookstove, which is going full blast. It is pressed into service for the pies and the duck. The kitchen table is laden, and arms are flying and flailing. The youngsters are impatient, reluctant to wait for the serving dishes to travel around, and adults are reaching over to help load plates. Then it is time for the grown-ups in the dining room.

I look at the huge table, the family's faces, and the talk with David flashes through my mind. I want to voice my thanks and start to speak, and stop myself, inhibited and tongue-tied. What I want to say might be sentimental, maudlin. Everyone is hungry and full of anticipation, and the food is steaming before us. We are more well mannered and restrained than the children, but anxious nevertheless. Then the serving dishes begin their rounds, the instant is gone, and I have remained mute.

Just as well. So long as I acknowledge my own thanks it should be sufficient. I have no liking for preaching as a rule . . . well, everyone to their own way, their own commitments. I can't do it for anyone else; no one can do it for me.

But I can't shake the feeling of a missed moment. It stays with me like a gnawed bone. I value the rich feast of freedom, as a youngster having lived in a society that was not free. I want to give thanks for that, even though some in the family mock me for waving the flag, even though *freedom* is a relative term and its practice is imperfect. I want to give thanks for the bounty of it all, the bounty of family, of health. The bounty of food: There having been times when that was not to be taken for granted. For the children coming into my life and into their own. There is so much.

Just as well I did not open my mouth. There is too much to be said for it even to be begun.

*   *   *

Now the snow is a universal highway through the woods, and there being one missed moment in recent memory, I do not allow this to become another.

All the accouterments of the winter world await, greet me. The familiar footprints in the snow pronounce whose turf I traverse: fox, rabbit, partridge, mouse. I see no sign of the big owl who has moved into the area, whose occasional hooting echoes across the trees. Some day this winter we may meet, some occasion I may see the marks of its wingtips as it swoops down to fetch a mouse.

The tips of the pine branches are already snowladen, the accumulation waiting for my exposed neck. Beneath my skis the snowlayer is still thin and sparse and occasional hummocks of frozen duff, of ice clumps, let me know that the time has yet to come when I can glide easily among the trees along familiar winter trails.

But it is a good initiation, a good welcoming of the winter as the snow and I get reacquainted, and I am glad that I did not pass up the moment.

I may very well belong to that legion of humanity that thinks of the right thing to say long afterward, who become tongue-tied at the Thanksgiving table. But this moment right now belongs to me, to my lifetime and my memories. Irrevocable and without regrets.

*   *   *

Overhead a bald eagle is flying low, coasting, hovering. It should not be here anymore. Migration is earlier as a rule. The bird skims the frozen lake, perhaps searching for open water. Then it wheels toward the river, which is still running freely and apt to provide fish.

I'm not the only one to occasionally miss the moment. It may be a universal characteristic. One that can lend itself to remedy.

My skis take me downhill slowly. I think I will skirt the bottom of the hill, take the path through the tall trees. That will be . . . what? Two kilometers? Three? A nice loop in the fabric of my life.

32 Getting Lost in the Woods

A letter arrives from an old friend hallooing across the years and the miles. We had been high school chums and stayed in touch while I was in the service and overseas, and then at different colleges. We had hitchhiked halfway across the continent to visit one another. As each of us married and had children that we visited back and forth. The visits came farther apart and our correspondence more sporadic. We became estranged by sharply differing views on the Vietnam War and did not write to each other or call, our last face-to-face meeting marred by a bitter argument. Then he reached across the chasm and telephoned and I wrote and we visited once again. Now we stay in touch. Neither of us wants to lose a friend; both of us cherish the values of long acquaintance, of shared lives, of deep attachment.

I will answer his long letter today. But first I will walk in the woods, collecting my thoughts, for our letters go beyond reports on family happenings as we discuss, debate, events of the day, portents of things to come. He is a historian of national note and has valuable insights into political events. I would never have predicted that this is what he would become when we were in high school and he was a strong, burly boy with football-player shoulders and a wrestler's chest contrasting to my then-puny frame.

I dress for the cold north wind, the snowcrusted ground, and set out through the pine plantation heading for the forest beyond, and then the marshes fringing the river.

It is a brisk, chilling walk. Before long there will be sufficient snow to ski this trail, but right now it has to be walked. I seek an accommodation with the wind from the north, trying to achieve a sort of détente, but all the compromise will have to be on my part. There is no sign the wind will abate.

"Keewaydin," I hum to myself, for the moment forgetting the Ojibwe word for *north wind*, and having to do with the word for *north*. "Keewaydin ahnung," I hum. *North star*. I am not likely to forget *ahnung*, my daughter's Indian name. Still blocking on the word for *north wind*, I sing mental variations on *keewaydin* and *ahnung* as I walk through the tagalder swamp, the hummocks frozen, dead reeds and grass poking through the slim snow. The mental exercise in mnemonics helps me memorize Ojibwe words and phrases, and I do this on occasion on my walks.

For once the river is frozen, but I know well enough not to walk on the ice, which is treacherously thin, undercut by currents. The creek tempts me, however, and I probe for a safe crossing over the deep silt bed. On the other side and uphill, the trail takes me into thick aspen and jackpine woods crowding the hills.

My sense of direction sometimes becomes befuddled while crossing swamps and marshes, or while ducking and weaving through thick woods. I circle a tangle of brush and, in avoiding the impediment, change directions without being aware of it. Soon I look for the familiar landmark and don't find it. That big white pine with the lightning streak arrowing down the trunk — what happened to it? Where did it go? It should be right here! But it isn't.

This is unsettling and, if allowed, frightening. The white pine is exactly where it has always been; I just happen to be in a different place than I thought I was.

All of us who spend time in the woods have had this happen repeatedly. One's state of mind determines whether we feel panic or just dismay, and how we work our way out of the predicament. I've felt them all at various times, running the gamut from a wry smile at my own stupidity to outright terror. And I've been reluctant to admit to my family that I've gotten turned around and momentarily lost in my own woods.

I didn't even admit it to Peggy on the occasion when she lost her way in the spruce and tamarack swamp and had to climb a tall tree to look for landmarks. We had gone looking for her and heard her yell and shout. We returned the shouts and she found her way to us.

"Lost?" I asked her with a superior grin. "I heard you yell."

"I didn't yell!"

We had all heard her. "Okay, okay, you didn't yell."

"I wasn't lost," she continues. "Knew exactly where I was. I just had to figure out a good way to the hill."

We all have our pride to protect. I safeguard mine by not admitting the episodes of confusion.

*   *   *

Now I shelter beneath the damaged white pine, still where it has been these many years, and begin to compose my letter to my friend. I often sift and winnow my thoughts before sitting down to scribe them:

"Those months, two years back, when your marriage foundered and appeared ruined forever, must have been a time of distress and torment for you. Isn't it strange that so many human relationships undergo these trials. What is there about our nature and makeup that enables us to overcome such difficulties at one time, and to succumb to them another? I am happy that you and your wife made the effort and engaged in the struggle to repair your relationship, to re-establish it. The last time I saw you both you seemed very close and comfortable with each other, but it was different from earlier times. How? A bit more regard, more respect for each other's needs? Tell me. Write to me about this, my friend; I care.

"It was this way between us, too, when the awful argument about Vietnam drove us apart. You were right, of course, with your historian's perspective, and I was wrong with my preoccupation with the immediate politics of it. And oh, how we mismanaged our anger, both of us, and struck out to hurt each other. Yet thank you for initiating the reconciliation, after allowing both of us the time to cool off."

My mind wanders to other friendships of the past, other acquaintances, which loom ever more important to me as the
hours, the days, the years pass by. They are *ahnung*, the stars
shining brightly to backlight my life, are the people I have
known: the friends, the intimates, acquired so easily when one
is young, then jettisoned as one or the other moves away, becomes embroiled in the daily grind.

I am not one who sends Christmas cards, or writes an annual
letter. Instead I try to stay in touch with the bright stars of a
lifetime, the landmarks of my pilgrimage. They are an unlikely
assortment scattered across the countryside. An environmentalist in California's desert who raises selukis. A psychiatric social
worker near Detroit. A poet in Minneapolis. A foundry worker
and union official in Wisconsin. My older sons, in their roving
ways, their children scribbling loves and kisses at the end of letters. The common denominator is love, the sharing of a brief or
longer time, of caring.

I begin my walk home to write my friend. The letter is important. It is a way of not getting lost in life, any more than one
wants not to get lost in the woods.

Keewadin nodin is *north wind*. It comes to mind on the way.

33 Through the Woods by Dogsled

"Hike!"

The team of seven sled dogs is trotting, pulling. I find myself in instant motion, unaware of any jolt or jerk. It is different than a horse-drawn conveyance where there is always a lunge of sorts as you get underway; you get used to it doing farmwork with horses, or working from the seat of a horse-drawn wagon or sleigh. Cocooned on the dogsled, one moment watching Jim untangle harnesses, the next finding ourselves in motion at ten miles an hour, there has seemed to be no transition between standstill and speed.

"Lean into the curve," Jim instructs from the runners where he stands behind me. "And don't stick out your hands!"

We swerve, career out of his drive onto the snow-packed country road, the dogs at a steady trot. Trails branch where the road ends and the team leader heads to the right.

"No, we're not going trapping," Jim yells. "Not the trapline today. Left!"

He applies the brake, the drag helping to persuade the dogs that they are not off on a twenty-, thirty-, forty-mile trek but just an "attitude run" through the woods. Just a romp to exercise and have a bit of fun.

It is a silent run through the forest, the teflon sled runners barely scuffing in the snow, the dogs noiseless, the harness not even creaking. We are a submarine running deep among the trees that arch over the trail making a tunnel. My mind wants to whisper its thoughts to itself—so pervasive is the silence.

"Like going on skis without the effort," Jim speaks up behind me, then, "Whoa. Stop." He applies the brake and the team comes to a halt. "I'm not mad at you," he pronounces, dismounting. "Your traces are tangled," he tells the dogs, unscrambling two harnesses. "If I get left behind you'll have to climb over the back and put on the brakes."

I think the last comment is directed at me. Jim keeps up a steady conversation with the dogs and I have to listen closely for any asides directed at me. I hope he does not get left behind. I do not relish the prospect of climbing over the high back of the sled while it is in motion at ten miles an hour, trees and brush reaching out from both sides, and applying a brake the whereabouts and mechanics of which I have as yet to discover.

* * *

The cold bites through my snowmobile suit, penetrates my mittens and gloves, but the dogs seem unaffected by it, pulling steadily and in unison, a true team.

"Something wrong with that rear dog's hind leg?" I ask. The animal seemed to favor one leg.

"The one on the right? He's all right. It's just his way; some dogs run like that."

Then, in a clearing, he halts the team again. This time there is no reassurance that he isn't mad. I check quickly for any offense I might have committed, can detect none, but Jim passes me and walks up to the team. He pets the lead dog, lets the alpha to lick his bearded chin, then walks around to the third dog on the right side.

"You've been laying back letting the others do the pulling," Jim scolds. He pulls off his huge, heavy mittens, gauntlets really, and whaps the dog over the head. This is more of a show of Jim's displeasure than inflicting of pain. Jim returns by way of the lead dog, who gets another petting, then yells "Hike!" before mounting his riding platform. Dogs, sled, and I take off at a great pace and I clutch the sides, hoping Jim can hop on. He does.

"I've got to let the leader lick my chin once in a while when the other dogs are watching," Jim explains. "He's the alpha, the leader, and he'll take care of any malingering when we get back." The chain of command had to be observed while on the trail; you can't undermine or ignore the leader, and Jim spends so much time with his team that he is part of it and sensitive to the nuances of relationships between the individual dogs that constitute the whole.

*　　*　　*

He traps, hunts, gardens in an effort at self-sufficiency.

"I'm not even going to drive a car anymore," Jim pronounces. "What the oil companies are doing is obscene, using profits to buy movie studios, publishing houses, television networks. You have to starve the oil companies by not buying their products, that's the only way."

I'm not entirely sure that Jim is totally serious about bringing Gulf Oil to its knees. But he is a great conversationalist and not about to let go of a good topic.

"I burn wood for heating and cooking, and next summer I'm getting a horse."

"To go to town? To shop?" Visions of the horse parked in the lot of First National Bank while he is inside, then at the supermarket.

"I've taken the dog team into town to go shopping," he sounds a bit defensive. "Worked just fine. Tied them near the railroad tracks in front of the Union Station. Took up two parking spaces there. All those people around and no one so much as gave it a second look."

My shoulders must have sagged in a way suggesting incredulity.

"If I had to, I could even canoe into town from my house," he continues. "It's only three-fourths of a mile from my door to Grant Creek." He explains the route and again there is a long silence.

"Well, it would take me a day and a half one way. . . . " he finally concedes. "But it could be done."

The sled speeds, the dogs setting a fearful pace.

"Getting close to home?" I ask.

"They smell a deer. They can go twenty-five miles an hour or better for short distances. But they'll keep right on going past the deer, even if it is standing next to the trail."

The lead dog picks a path around a fallen tree, avoiding a tangle of brush. Then we are out of the woods, going down a trail skirting fields, approaching the homestead.

"Hold on! Lean into the curve! Sometimes we tip over here!"

It is a wild turn into the yard and we come to a stop in an open area where the dogs are tied to their stakes, each one to their own little bit of turf and shelter.

*   *   *

"How did you like your first ride?" Jim's wife, Sarah, asks. "On my first ride I knocked down the mailbox."

"She stuck out her arm," Jim explains.

"Did you get hurt? Break the arm?"

"No, it wasn't much of a mailbox. But he hit me over the head with his mittens."

"Well what did you expect me to do? Kiss you with the whole team looking on?"

34 Youth: To Learn and To Grow

The girl is beautiful and I cannot believe it. What happened to the chubby, saucer-eyed, earnest babysitter? Who pouted, having to help her mother can garden vegetables? Who feuded with brothers and younger sister in a nonstop squabble? Who perpetually bulged over, around, and inside the skintight blue jeans? Who slopped through 4-H meetings and exhibits and projects, planing the surface of effort?

This girl is glamorous, stunning, and she looks out of place at the 4-H party and dance.

"Put your eyes back in their sockets," my wife advises as she passes, coffee pot in one hand, cookie plate in the other.

"She's wearing makeup," I say, half to myself, for I have been left behind in a cloud of disapproval. "And she's lost weight. This is a beautiful young woman, no longer a girl."

Others have noticed the metamorphosis, the emergence of the gorgeous butterfly from the chrysalis, and comment on it.

The dancing begins. She moves gracefully. She will be a very striking young woman, I think. Then I see something, a flash, but I am sure that I am not mistaken.

The youngsters are dancing, the individualized gyrations of yesteryear's rock giving way to the clutching couples and pseudoembrace of two decades ago. The music is slower, more melodic too. Feet are shuffling, more or less in unison, and the girl is holding her partner tightly about the neck, while he has one arm firmly around her waist. As they turn in slow-motion pirouette, I see her face clearly. Her eyes are glazed, the lips parted, she is breathing heavily, rapidly. The image under the strobe light of the moment is one of sexual arousal. Then I lose sight in the moil of the couples.

It is the age, of course, of intensified curiosity, preoccupation with sex, at a time when so many youngsters are most inhibited when talking about it. I have no way of knowing how open her parents are to discussing it, or how aware and sensitive they are.

I wish myself into an imaginary conversation wherein I could tell her: Yes, it is a difficult time. You are growing up and searching for a sense of yourself, of who you are. And when all has been said to you that can be said by parents and teachers about reproduction, and pregnancy, and premature marriage, then there is still that indefinable aspect that no young person ever wants to acknowledge. It is sometimes called maturity. Human sexuality is the primary, basic expression of one individual saying to another: This is who I am, this is me—I am sharing my self with you. Impossible, isn't it, to say this until you have a sense of who you are? And unfortunately experiments, and satisfaction of curiosity, before one has gained that acceptance and knowledge of oneself, can do a lot of damage to the very process of finding oneself. A paradox: A body at fruition conjoined to an unripe psyche.

The girl is among a cluster of friends at the punchbowl and cookie table. She is nattering with the rest, the femme fatale of a minute ago once again fifteen, a youngster in a 4-H dress having a good time. Of course I won't speak to her; one can't just engage a comparative stranger in such personal talk. And also, I have found out in trying to discuss such matters with my older children, when they were in their teens, that it is difficult to talk about human sexuality beyond the biological and mechanical levels, beyond the levels of ethics and morality, to the question of maturity and the ingredient of honesty in such a personal relationship. I still recall the look of puzzlement on my children's faces when I tried to explain that anything less brings with it the risk of exploitation and of degradation. They didn't know what I was talking about.

It is so easy for a young person to be sexually exploited, degraded, through one's own unwitting actions—and unfortunately through the actions of others, often elders. It is much more common than one thinks, than I used to think. And it is usually not the stranger offering treats who lures the youngster, but someone known, someone within the family circle. It happened to me when I was a very young child, about four I think, and a babysitter long on good will but short on common sense used the occasion to satisfy her curiosity about the subject. I was so bewildered and abashed that I did not dare tell my parents, yet the experience obviously disturbed me for a long time.

Later, a twelve-year-old refugee being handed from one set of strangers to another, alone and cut off from family, I was sexually abused by an adult. Helpless, with no one to turn to, I felt overwhelmed by anger and frustration, and then—inexplicably—by a feeling of guilt, as though I had been, in some unknowable way, responsible, a perpetrator and not a victim.

It was only years later that it began to dawn on me, reading and hearing about the experiences of others, that it is common for youngsters not to tell anyone, that such crimes are rarely reported. It is also common for the victim to turn the guilt and shame upon oneself. And sad to say, it is also common to turn the anger against one's parents for not protecting one.

Reason alone tells me that my father and mother could not have protected me from either occasion; at the time that I was twelve my father was still trying to escape the Nazis and concentration camp, and my mother was working as a live-in domestic far away, working from daybreak to nightfall, and prohibited from having me stay with her. Yet it required years for me to work out, to resolve my feelings about these things, and they delayed and retarded my emotional and spiritual maturing.

I sometimes think that I was a less than good partner, husband, parent, simply because I had never told anyone, had never cleared my mind and spirit of these events, had never cleansed my emotional house of the warping darkness that had intruded there.

I look now at the lovely girl at the 4-H party, at my own children grown and growing, and I cannot help wondering if evil has befallen, or will befall, despite my own best efforts. I know with sadness that I cannot protect them from everything in life, try as I might, and that in the final analysis all I can do is to keep the channels of communication open, to keep myself available, so that if and when it does, they will share with me and allow me to help.

I can rear my children to the best of my ability, I can be aware and open, and try to instruct, and be an example. So that if it should befall them to be tested and tried they will have the inner strength and the trust in themselves and in my love and respect of them to share.

One last look at the young girl, overnight grown swan from duckling. It must be particularly difficult for a young woman to be pretty, to be beautiful, and thereby become an object of attention: an object, not a growing, sentient human being. Our society, with its emphasis on sexuality in advertising, which broaches on pornography at times, and on physical endowments and measurements, does a great disservice in this regard. And the primary victim is the youngster, usually the girl, but also the boy, growing up and concerned with inward life, subjected to attention to the outer.

We leave and I wave goodbye to the folks, to the girl and her parents, and others. I wish her well.

I have my own little girl in my arm and she is huddling against me in the brisk air. With my other arm I give one of the bigger boys a hug.

"That was nice. What was it for?" he asks.

"Just because."

"Because what?"

"Because I love you. Here are the keys, start the car for me, will you, while I put the little one in the back seat?"

35 Getting a Home is a Moving Experience

There is a less than exorbitant solution to the cost of housing in small towns and rural areas. It isn't cheap by any means, and the dream house is conditioned by reality, but the final product costs a fraction of conventional construction. The longstanding, obscure method is called *house moving*. It is a time-honored American practice born of necessity and practicality.

Just before the turn of the century, a gold rush at Rainy Lake, on the U.S.-Canadian border, saw the overnight birth of a town of hundreds of people. Some of the sudden settlers had traveled west to east in covered wagons to get in on the bonanza, others had come overland, and sawmills and gold stamping mills were hauled cross-country in excruciating frenzy to get rich quickly. There was not nearly as much gold as had been hoped, the town died, another community, now known as International Falls, sprang up about a dozen miles away to take advantage of hydroelectric power harnessed from Koochiching Falls. The new town used the building materials, and in some instances, the very buildings of the old: Jack up the building, slide skids under it, lower the building onto the skids, and away we go.

Also around the turn of the century, a whole community had sprung up outside the boundary of the Leech Lake Indian Reservation in Minnesota. When squatters, railroads, and the government succeeded in breeching the Indian lands, the off-reservation town of Ferris saw many of its buildings and most of its inhabitants move a half dozen miles east to become today's village of Cass Lake.

American mobility and ingenuity combined with Yankee parsimony to give birth to a time-saving approach to construction. The practice is alive and well today.

*   *   *

"I've had it, living in a trailer," she announces. She has said it before, but somehow he senses that this time there is a firmness, an obstinate determination to it. The tone of voice suggests that there is an "or else" lurking in the background, and he does not want to find out the precise nature of the threat.

"Okay, okay, I'll go talk to the Jamisons."

"Today, and I'm coming with you."

The Jamisons are a hardworking clan who keep much to themselves. They log, operate a sawmill, a lumberyard, and sell and move old houses. One plot of their sprawling enclave is given over to a wild array of structures no longer wanted by erstwhile owners: a two-car garage, a small warehouse, a gingerbread two-story clapboard house, a huge and rambling lodge once the centerpiece of a famous resort, a one-story family home with a sleeping loft. Any type of structure, of whatever period and design, could sooner or later be found at the Jamisons. The building would be jacked up, resting on crisscrossed timbers, and waiting in line for the prospective buyer like certain girls in an old western saloon.

Stories abound about the Jamisons: They belong to an obscure religious group (not true; some of them attend one of the largest churches in the community); they are all bachelors (some are, others have large families and the clan is continually expanding). What is true is that the Jamisons march to their own drummer, to a music that no one else can hear.

They accept jobs and reject others on a formula no one has yet fathomed, and show up to do the work unexpectedly, usually long after a purchaser has given up on ever seeing them. They then go about their work in a seemingly chaotic way, Jamisons clambering all about the place like ants on a disturbed hill, ramshackle trucks and tractors strewn about the area, which is also littered with a wild assortment of timbers and paraphernalia, chains, cables, and jacks. Then they are gone as suddenly as they have come, every bit of litter picked up, and that old building has vanished, or a building has been moved in.

*   *   *

"I don't like any of them," she says defiantly. They have been clambering in and out of the Jamisons' current assortment, and she is brushing dust and dirt off her clothes.

The three Jamisons accompanying them look at each other but say nothing. Taciturnity is their strong suit; perhaps they have found it to be good salesmanship, because when they are at work moving a house they are garrulous.

"D'you see the ones back there?" a Jamison finally allows, nodding in the direction behind the lumberstacks and sawdust pile.

There are three more houses there.

"Look," she exclaims, "there are some old blue mason jars in here. I want them. And look, this would be perfect, we could put the kids up here, make some nice little bedrooms, and put a dormer over there. . . ."

He stares in disbelief. The wallpaper is peeling, there are cracks, holes in the plaster. Portions of the sill have rotted, the clapboard siding is curled, and he suspects that the roof is not all that good either.

"Used to be the Goodrich house," a Jamison says. "Had to move it to make way for the shopping mall."

She has found her house.

"But honey, those sills have to be replaced on the north side!"

"Not too bad," a Jamison says, "especially if you do it while we have it jacked up."

"You can do it!" Her confidence in the husband is overwhelming, the smile radiant.

"That roof doesn't look too good. . . ." He is fighting a losing battle and knows it.

"You did such a good job on the roof on your mom's house!"

"It needs a little work but it's a good, solid house, that Goodrich house," a Jamison says with deadly timing. "Still cost you a fraction of just the lumber alone, if you was to build from scratch."

They agree on price, on time of delivery. "Now that's if we don't have to have the telephone or power company come and move overhead wires on the way, that'll be extra," Jamisons warn.

"And you'll have the driveway smooth and wide enough," another Jamison cautions. "And you'll let us know as soon as you have the basement in, so we can set it down."

The wife is clutching the grimy blue canning jars as they get in their car, homeowners at last—almost.

*   *   *

"The basement's been in three weeks," she says over the phone. "When are you going to bring our house?"

"They left early this morning to move a forestry building from Blackduck," the female voice answers. "Don't know when they'll be back, probably late tonight."

"Will you give them a message?"

"I will if I see them. But this is Simon's, and he doesn't move houses. He sells lumber. You want Jeremiah."

"What's his phone?"

"Doesn't have one."

She drives to the Jamison compound at night, but they have not yet returned. Early the next morning she is back, and the whole clan is loading its caravan of ancient trucks, bulldozers, timbers, and gear on the way to another project.

"Can't do it today," a Jamison calls over his shoulder. "We'll try tomorrow or next. . . ."

A week later she employs a new stratagem. Dawn finds her sitting on the doorstep of the bachelors' cottage, knitting.

"What are you doing here?" the emerging Jamison protests.

The other bachelor brother is stunned: "Hey, young lady, you can't be sitting here! What will people say?" The cottage is visible from the highway.

"I want my house moved!"

*   *   *

They watch the Jamison caravan approaching, lumbering, stopping while one leaps out of a truck, grasps a twenty-foot-long pole, pushes up a sagging telephone wire hanging across the road.

"Go ahead," he yells, "chimney's clear."

Their new home approaches, stops again at the turn into the driveway.

"Got to take down the fenceposts, can't make the turn," a Jamison announces, chain saw in hand.

"Those trees are pretty close too, may have to take them down," another is eyeing the drive.

"Not my trees!" she protests. "I planted every one of them!"

Jamisons seem to shrug their shoulders in unison. The fence comes down, but ropes are thrown around the treetops, and the pines are pulled backward, more flexible than one would have thought, and none have to be sawed. The trees spring upright after the house passes. It is resting on a huge, low-slung bed that rolls on countless wheels, pulled by a snorting, huffing truck that looks like a period piece from World War I. A crew-cab pickup truck loaded with gear has preceded, and another truck with a bulldozer follows, as do two cars disgorging Jamisons. Within minutes strewn timbers and gear cover the area around the brand-new basement.

"Will they set it down and move it on the basement?" she asks her husband.

An army of Jamisons builds trestles of crisscrossed timbers, virtually filling the basement. The gigantic dolly carrying the house is backed onto the temporary trestle-road, the house is jacked up, the dolly pulled out.

The house now floats a few inches above its new basement, hovers there, as she bites her knuckles. The men push, shove, tug; chains are hooked from the house to one of the trucks, a winch tightens them, moving the house one inch, another.

"A little bit north yet," a Jamison calls. Another set of winches, another truck. They nurse, nudge the building into precise alignment with the basement.

"Put in your sill sealer," a Jamison says, "and we'll set her down."

*   *   *

"Watch out now!" he calls to the clambering, exploring children. "There are loose boards, you be careful!"

"It's their new home, let them look around," she pleads.

He thinks of the terrible work ahead, the demolishing and rebuilding, replastering and painting; of the new siding and roofing, the wiring and plumbing, and is aghast at what they are undertaking.

"At least we have our own home, and we can pay for it," she says. "We don't have to do it all at once."

But he knows that with each passing day the pressures will mount to move out of the mobile home and into the more spacious house, whether it is done or not.

"Look over here, somebody left this old easy chair!" she calls from one of the rooms.

It is dirty, dilapidated, the only furnishing.

"No wonder they left it, but it looks comfortable."

"Here, you sit in it," she tries to comfort him.

A cloud of dust rises, billows, envelopes him, one of the legs creaks a warning.

"I'll fix it," she promises, "reupholster . . . paint. . . ." She is trying to read his quizzical expression.

"Oh well," he says, trying to rise from the enfolding chair and dust cloud, "be it ever so humble. . . ."

The sound of falling plaster from upstairs.

"Guess the kids have started to work," he grins. "Might as well join them."

36 What the Twins Told the Tax Assessor

Omens and superstitions are ridiculous vestiges of the times before the scientific revolution. We know now that the future can not be foretold by examining the viscera of sacrificial lambs, and coincidentally we have discovered that a good leg of lamb does more for us anyhow. But somehow life is full of the vestiges of the folk tales that, like appendixes, sometimes act up. And admit it or not, we all have a few nervous spots on our psyches that, under proper circumstances and stimulation, discomfit us.

My wife has such a spot where owls are concerned. Some grandmother in her life had told her, when she was little, that an owl flying over you was a sign of death, and consequently owls are not welcome at our place.

Some years ago this particular superstition caused distress when, on a late afternoon walk, an owl started circling over my head, and ultimately dive-bombed me. This was no longer a matter subject to interpretation (in other words, did the owl actually fly over you, or only nearby? This one had singled me out from the rest of humanity, and from among the several of us in the walking party).

"It's nothing personal," I pant, in the middle of evasive action, as the infuriated owl dives at me again and I note the look of anguish on my wife's face. "He has taken a dislike to my red beret."

I duck behind a tree and the owl, momentarily baffled, roosts on a branch overhead.

"You're not wearing your beret!"

"Maybe it's because I haven't washed my hair lately." I grasp at straws, saying anything just to keep her from being terrified. Myself as well. Who knows, maybe there is something to the old superstition.

I start out again, and the owl resumes the attack, coasting inches above my hair. We arrive home out of breath in a dead heat, shoving to get inside first as the owl takes a triumphant swoop over the house.

A naturalist friend laughs and says it has happened to him, that the owl is just protecting its nest and territory.

"But it's not nesting season any more," I point out, "and it only picks on me. Never on the kids, who pass by there daily, or on Peggy. Just me."

"Maybe there's something about you that annoys that owl," he says. It is a lame excuse and I worry.

"Are you feeling all right?" my wife asks. She is unusually solicitous.

*   *   *

When four years have passed without a fatality my wife decides that while the superstition about owls may be correct, my experience was an aberrant one, something aside and apart from the norm of omens. Owls are still not welcome to fly over the house, it's just that the one that hates me doesn't know his business.

*   *   *

I can laugh about her superstitions, but I take mine seriously. This morning I know that the day will be a disaster. Never mind how I know, I've had the sign.

"You be good now, Daddy'll be back in a moment," I tell the twins. There are times in one's life that require prompt response and brook no interference. "Eat your cereal now," I admonish as I depart.

They are silent. From the bathroom I hear nothing until the quiet is punctuated by shrill, insane laughter. First Micah, then Megan. What can children who are not yet three find so funny?

They laugh again, and shriek. How nice, I think, they are playing.

Indeed, they are playing. I find them on the kitchen table. Megan has emptied the rice cereal box on the table and is molding a huge mountain, while Micah is sending sprays of cereal throughout the kitchen with a spatula.

I say something vehement. It comes from the heart, and as the words pour out I know that I will regret it. I do already. Micah and Megan will repeat the expletives when we have company.

"Did you drop the cereal box?" my wife asks on entering the kitchen, smothering a smile while I smother her with a look.

"Hey, Tony, look, Dad spilled a whole bunch of cereal! Bye, Dad!" They are in their rite of passage to the school bus and cannot be delayed to help.

"I hope your teachers really sock it to you today!" I shout after them.

"Got to go now," says Peggy. "Jury trial today."

*　　　*　　　*

"Got to go now," says the babysitter. "My boyfriend is home from the Air Force and . . . Oh, I forgot to tell you. Your wife called to say not to wait supper. The jury's still out and she's going to be home late."

I've known all along it would be bad. I had the omen in the morning.

Megan beats me to the front door to greet the stranger who knocks—pretty, blonde, blue-eyed, petite Megan, my one and only daughter with the face of an angel and the clarion voice of Liza Doolittle.

"Hello, I'm your tax assessor—oh, what a charming little girl!"

"Get out!" orders Megan, at her imperial worst. Other people's two-year-olds lisp; why can't mine?

"Come in, come in," I try to compensate for Megan's hostility.

The tax assessor looks dubious, enters cautiously, and we sit at the kitchen table going over house dimensions.

"No, no, that's not a room over there," I protest, "that's an atrium, part of our solar heating system. Come out there, I'll show you."

We open the sliding glass door to the atrium and I show the tax assessor how the solar heating works when there is an ominous click behind us. Megan has enlisted Micah, their grinning faces are glued to the glass doors. They have locked us in the atrium.

My gestures, shouts, threats avail nothing. Megan and Micah think them hilarious. Tony and David are out of earshot. The tax assessor and I are firmly locked into the solar heating system.

David finally finds us and unlocks the door.

"Hot out there," I am wiping perspiration, only partially engendered by the eighty-two-degree temperature.

We resume our seats about the kitchen table. Supper is beginning to scorch and I leap to the stove to turn things down.

"This won't be taking much longer," the tax assessor assures me, "and I've been trying to catch up with you for some time. . . ."

The twins are ominously quiet and I spy them behind our guest. They have managed to get into the one-foot space between a double set of sliding glass doors opening from kitchen to the barbecue deck, and close the doors again. There they are, like goldfish in a bowl. Megan is removing her clothes, Micah is beginning to emulate her.

I make discouraging signs with my hands, trying to pay attention to the tax assessor and answer questions, yet somehow dissuade my little strippers. They are not to be stopped. They know with a sure and certain instinct when they are immune.

Naked now. Both. I hope the tax assessor will continue to look at *me* with gimlet eyes and ask more questions, and will not turn around. There is a peal of hysterical laughter. Megan is tickling Micah. More shrieks and guffawing, and the visitor turns to see what is going on. The naked twins perform with gusto.

Megan shouts (expletive deleted). She is repeating my outburst from the morning's cereal episode, once again enunciating clearly. She ends the recital, which has been delivered with real feeling, and smiles sweetly. My angel! Just wait until I get my hands on you!

"I've never been in a household quite like this," the assessor says after a longish pause. "I think I've got all that I need and will turn this over to the county treasurer. Maybe he'll come out here himself."

I hope to have a good omen on the day the tax bill arrives but have little expectation of it. Scientific method has surely overtaken superstition where science holds sway, but the only method in my life is madness.

"Megan? Micah? Where are you? Where have those children disappeared to now?"

37 The Life You Save

Holiday traffic was heavy and the highway shimmered in the heat when the pickup truck swerved suddenly, slowed on the shoulder, and then made a quick U-turn. The driver doubled back a few hundred yards and then parked on the opposite shoulder. He got out while wife and children watched and walked to the middle of the highway, standing guard and waving aside traffic from both directions. The snapping turtle scrabbled across the hot concrete toward the swamp. Turtles move faster than one would expect, and this one was quickly in the safety of the swamp.

Life is sacred to traditional Indians and symbolic or spiritual values are represented by everything in creation. The holiday traveler was saving the life of one snapping turtle on its way home from laying eggs in the sand dunes, and he was saving something more besides.

We all want to be heard, we all want linkage with the great mystery of creation, whether we worship with incense in a church, post sacred scrolls on our doorjambs, or put pictures or little altars in our homes. Some of us who profess to be agnostics, skeptics, or disbelievers find the linkages in other ways. Yet few forms of our search for spirituality are so strongly linked to every form and manifestation of creation as those of traditional American Indians.

The code word here is *Traditional*. Even before Christian missionaries came to subvert native religion, not every Indian was able or willing to subscribe to the high moral tenets and requirements of the Indian religious teachings, any more so than people in Christian cultures. Indians fought tribal wars while

Catholics fought Protestants—and the teachings of both Indians and Christians upheld the sanctity of life.

The man who saved the turtle watched it disappear into the swamp. He reached into a pocket and drew out a small tobacco pouch, extracting a handful, which he offered to the sky before depositing it at the edge of the grass. It was his mark of respect, his offering to be part of the whole, his witness for spirituality—even though it was hot and the traffic was fast, and he and his family were as anxious as all other travelers to get home, or the swimming beach, or a family picnic.

On a hot June Sunday, one man stood in the middle of a highway and said that he cared enough about his own life to save the life of a turtle.

38 The Sagging Barn

The old, hipped roof barn invites a visit, lonely and isolated in the neglected pasture. It is still a faded red, probably painted last long ago with lead base paint, and the trim is still white, suggesting a faint odor of chalk. But the great drop-door of the hayloft is long gone. It should be open, and a crew of boys and farmhands should be pitching fresh hay into the far corners, stacking it well, as the fork hoists up a new load from the wagon below, the thick rope creaking on the pulleys someone forgot to grease. It smells so good, that fresh hay, it almost makes you forget the chaff tickling your nose.

But the hayloft door is gone and most window panes have disappeared. The rooster weather vane still presides nobly over the peak, but the roof below is full of holes, letting in rain and snow, and the deck of the hayloft is spongy and rotten in spots. If you dare climb up into the empty hayloft, stepping gingerly where the boards look solid and there is a good chance of some half-solid joists below, you can see down through the holes in the floor into the milking parlor. And there—on the other side—are the horse stalls. And—look—a few old stanchions are left, and a couple of drinking cups in the cow parlor. And—here—a few pieces of metal track hanging from the ceiling. A gondolalike container used to coast along that track, into the milking parlor for the farmer or his youngster to pitch in manure; then it would be pulled out the side door and dumped on a heap to compost and later would be spread in the field.

But the compost heap has decomposed and turned into rich black soil, and the fields are empty except for the weeds and a few scraggly, encroaching jackpine where the oats used to wave at the wind in friendly greeting. Or was it the wind waving at the oats?

Oh yes, here is where the pigs were penned. And over there a few pieces of harness are still hanging from the nails on the wall. The leather is dry and cracked, and coated with dust.

A date in the cement floor of the milking parlor: 1927. Did they build the barn then? It looks old enough to have been . . . No, look at that! The inside walls are solid logs! In the dim light you can see the chop marks—they are hand-hewn. This was built long before 1927; it was just the cement work that was added then. And the shiplap siding, that must have come later, too, because the logs are still chinked with white plaster.

How sturdy and promising it must have looked when it was new, all hewn logs and fresh white chinking, rising among the newly cleared fields rolling over the gentle hills. What daring was here, after how many long months and years of felling and milling the trees, and maybe a workbee or two to build it. And what will happen to it now, empty and disintegrating in the weather? Will anyone come along and say, "You are a monument to courage and to hard work, and there is beauty in your lines and in your old, hard-labored wood, I won't let you die"? Now who would say such a thing? There is no money in the farming, and there is little or no use for such a building, and it is sad to think of the lives played out to build it, to use it, and now nothing to show for it.

When you walk away a distance to look back at the whole of it sitting in its tiny little swale of a long-ago farmyard, you begin to notice the old pieces of farm machinery rusting in the once-upon-a-time fields. A couple of hay wagons, only the steel wheels peeking over the top of the grass and weeds. A plow, two twelve-inchers. Corn picker. Hay rake. Cultivator. Binder. Mower with the sickle bar pointing up at the sky, a few blades still intact.

Your memory ear still hears the farmer instructing the boy: "Never stand in front of the sickle bar when you're unplugging it. Those horses twitch or move, and you lose your feet."

And you hear the wife calling out: "Lunch!" which is a snack in the middle of the forenoon, because at noon it will be dinner.

And right now you are alone in the field, looking at the barn, and it's just a memory. The smells, the sounds, they belong to the long ago.

Each rusty piece of machinery was bought with a loan, a new mortgage on the place and a new pressure to work harder, to make the place pay. The courthouse records will show the loans, the satisfactions, the new loans, the new hopes and fears and efforts until that final one that was never paid off. Were they tired by then? Worn out? Did the kids leave for work in the cities? Did the soil get so poor it cost more in fertilizer than the crops brought in?

It feels disrespectful to walk away from the old barn and to let it sink into further ruin. It is saddening to witness so helplessly the end of something that was so good. So hard, yes, but still, so good.

A groundhog peers out from beneath the threshold that the farmer crossed many times daily in the course of the chores and watches you leave. Inside, the bats and squirrels cease their scrabblings and settle down again.

Turning for that last look, the log barn with the shiplap siding and the great hipped roof still seems sturdy, but you have been inside and know better. And you walk away thinking of the people who lived and worked there, and what it was like when they walked away for the last time, wishing it didn't have to be so but no longer having any other choices left.

Goodbye, old barn. Goodbye, way of life.

39 Winter's Blanket Toss

"Who has my hat? Hey, that's mine!"

"Do I *have* to wear snowpants? Why, Mom?"

And where did the goggles go? And those leggings? And who stole the laces out of the ski boots?

When a large family, numbers swelled by holiday guests, prepares to go cross-country skiing there is inevitable confusion, heightened by a small amount of anxiety. That certain downhill run is waiting for Mom; she claims she always falls down at the same spot (it has a personal grudge against her). And small Brother is wondering what the big one will say when, passing the winter campsite, he discovers that the little one had used up the whole pile of firewood. Everyone has his own private concerns, and in combination it makes for noise and confusion until the front door spurts the disorderly two-leggeds, like champagne bubbling out of a bottle.

Once in the woods the winter silence, helped by a few uphill and downhill turns in the trail, changes the raucous crowd into a quiet one. We distance from each other, not so much from the vigorous pace as the desire to connect with the winter world. Cold gusts come unexpectedly, sucking away breath momentarily. A snow-covered hazel branch traps a ski-tip. But by and large the skiing trip becomes a very private, solitary journey into winter.

Here is Mother Earth, sleeping beneath her thick, white winter blanket. She is resting, gathering strength for the great burst of spring energy, for the birthing and the growing. She is a fecund force and there are reminders of it all about. Next spring's buds have already formed on the tips of branches, guarded by their own little blankets of husk. Deer have crossed the ski trail, but in the deep snow it is difficult to tell how fresh the tracks are. Near the river are coyote tracks emerging from the trees and searching for open water, the bellies plowing shallow grooves in the top of the snow while the legs and footpads sink down. And always, there is the north wind, cleansing the world even as it chills, sweeping swirls of snow before it.

The movement of legs, of arms, of skis, becomes automatic after a while and less of a conscious effort. Up, down, moving atop the blanket. I am an Inuit in a blanket toss, thrown up to the sky, falling down into the folds, whirling up again, moved by forces beyond my control, my spirit cleansed by the north wind as is the earth.

Mother Earth's winter blanket is here for me, too, if I am willing to be part of the life cycle and to relish the living of it. Let me be tossed in winter's blanket! Let me be part of the powerful process of life, not merely a passive bystander. So what if the wind sweeps away my breath and I gasp; so what if I will never win the Finlandia Ski Race or be the graceful skier shown on television ads.

We return home minutes apart, shedding gear and hanging the outer clothing in the furnace room to dry. Our faces tingle from the collision between body heat and cold air. We are not so noisy now, and I glance out the window as the last stragglers plod into the yard.

An Ojibwe prayer says: "Thank you, Mother Earth, for sharing your winter blanket with us." And Simon and Garfunkel sang: "Life, I love you, all is groovy."

40 Beavers Teach Yet Another Lesson

In my woods as in my life there are times when I push away from the table, so to speak, to gain a sense of perspective, of distance, and of time. This is occasioned once again by the beavers.

They are emerging from the shrinking ice pan over the lake, hungry for fresh food, the winter stores waterlogged and diminishing. Once again the assorted trappers have failed to live up to their promises; once again the beavers have multiplied handsomely. Once again I eschew, I shy away from Draconian measures.

"I know you've got problems," the game warden says. "I can blow the dam for you."

We both know the beavers usually rebuild the dam.

The game warden could shoot them, if need be. They are vulnerable on land but shooting ruins the fur. He could blow up the lodge, the detonation killing adults and newborns alike. It seems a gross and wasteful act.

Yet they forage further, widening their menu from aspen to birch and even willow. With the flowage impeded, the lake is becoming more eutrophic: more plant growth in it, consequently more oxygen depletion as the plants die in winter, the oxygen consumed by the dying vegetation, aquatic life including fish diminishing.

This spring I cannot muster wry humor at my own expense. The annual re-emergence for once is not a conversation piece, a device from which I hang funny anecdotes. It leads instead to a pensive assessment.

There is a clump of birch in my vista of which I have become fond over the years, bare beacons in winter, in spring first pale and lush green thereafter, waver of bright yellow flags in fall. The clump is dead, flooded out and drowned? Gnawed? I have no interest in hiking over to look, it is pointless. Whatever the cause, the landmark is gone.

Were I living in town, the atrophy of a yard tree would be a significant event. Here in the woods where the natural processes and cycles wend their way, trees die and come into being in profusion, even if a familiar passes away.

How would I have felt had I lived here a few thousand years ago, as people have for close to 12,000 years — since the last glacier disappeared? And as they, in all likelihood, did during the warm millennia before the last glacier was formed? Landscape and climate would have been similar, and most wildlife the same; there would have been no white-tailed deer, instead there would have been caribou, elk, and moose. Otherwise trees and vegetation, flowers, wildlife, fish would have been much the same.

My life would have been keyed to the seasonal moieties. I could have lived where I do now in the winter months, moved to the maple sugar camp in early spring, before breakup. From there I would probably have gone to a village site for the summer-gathering and gardening, and fishing; perhaps at Ravens Point on Winnibigoshish. In late summer, after berrying, I would have headed for the wild rice beds, then back to the winter camp. One summer I might have joined others for the long trip to Isle Royale to dig copper. One winter, game being scarce, I might have taken the family over to Red River and down to the Assiniboine, then up that river to hunt and trap. One hungry spring I might have left the family at sugar camp to join a few other men on a trip to the prairies, three or four days west, to look for buffalo.

Then strangely, inexplicably, the weather turns warmer. Year by year the boreal forest gives way to encroaching prairie. The thick, tall grasses travel eastward across the Red River, into Minnesota, spreading in spots and tongues into Wisconsin.

As prairie spreads and forest retreats, elk and caribou are re-placed by buffalo. There are undulating hills now, with grasses wafting in the wind. Periodic fires sweep the countryside and consume the dead, matted vegetation, and help buried seeds to germination in the rains that follow. From a hilltop I could see afar.

Then strangely, inexplicably, the climate changes back. The prairie retreats, the forest returns. Back also are caribou, elk, and moose. Gone, with a few exceptions, are the buffalo.

I would not have been Methuselah and would not have seen it all, even though the change from start to finish required but a few hundred years. Yet even in a normal lifetime, the amount of change for a person living in one place must have been stag-gering and bewildering.

*   *   *

Change today is no less massive. I am middle-aged, yet I have seen the advent of the nuclear age, have witnessed the pro-gression from the zeppelins and biplanes of my childhood to space travel, lasers, and cybernetics. My wife's memory and ex-perience spans kerosene light and wood stove cooking to pas-sive solar heating. The explosion of knowledge, as of popula-tion and consequent human stress, is unprecedented, the future as unknown as it would have been in this place ten thousand years ago.

What have we, then, to guide us, beyond the daily mechanics of existentialism? A respect for the basic processes of nature, a respect for the land that its regenerative systems be not de-stroyed or altered. An acceptance of spirituality and ethics re-quired to make us and our relationships wholesome.

There are times when it seems we accomplish little, that we cannot manage things as we wish. We cannot get others to do as we wish; we cannot even get ourselves into harness. And the fulfillment of our hopes and desires seems remote and illusory; to even think of them is a galling reminder of what cannot be.

We all have dreams of glory, expectations of others, expecta-tions of ourselves.

The problem with the beavers is that I wish for the return of wildlife to the acreage I have stewarded on my terms. And my terms happen to be unrealistic.

It is a problem not of beavers, but of myself. I could be rid of them easily enough but am unwilling to compromise my sense of obligation and indebtedness to nature and creation. Therefore I must work on myself, my impractical expectations and wishes, and amend my desires. We do receive so much in life, and it is not always precisely what we have wanted, or when we have wanted it, so we do not accept it when it comes.

My acceptance comes from the here and the now, rather than the yesterday or the morrow. It comes from a knowledge and a love of the land and its ways. From consideration of prairie displacing pine forests long ago and the ultimate return of the trees.

It comes from the refreshing letter from a long silent friend, the unexpected hug. From my willingness to love and be loved, my acknowledgment of the needs of others as of my own. And it comes from the place in my life of the responsibilities as a social creature, lest our society becomes atomized.

And I suppose it comes from the ability to appreciate the clarity and beauty of sunrise that I may meet my inevitable sunset with equanimity and grace. For the life I live is but a loan, entrusted to my stewardship briefly, and the degree of my reward from this trust is filtered by the quality of my caretaking.

I will let the beavers be.